MongoDB Topology Design

Scalability, Security, and Compliance on a Global Scale

Nicholas Cottrell

Apress®

MongoDB Topology Design: Scalability, Security, and Compliance on a Global Scale

Nicholas Cottrell
St-Aubin-sur-Mer, France

ISBN-13 (pbk): 978-1-4842-5816-3   ISBN-13 (electronic): 978-1-4842-5817-0
https://doi.org/10.1007/978-1-4842-5817-0

Copyright © 2020 by Nicholas Cottrell

This work is subject to copyright. All rights are reserved by the Publisher, whether the whole or part of the material is concerned, specifically the rights of translation, reprinting, reuse of illustrations, recitation, broadcasting, reproduction on microfilms or in any other physical way, and transmission or information storage and retrieval, electronic adaptation, computer software, or by similar or dissimilar methodology now known or hereafter developed.

Trademarked names, logos, and images may appear in this book. Rather than use a trademark symbol with every occurrence of a trademarked name, logo, or image we use the names, logos, and images only in an editorial fashion and to the benefit of the trademark owner, with no intention of infringement of the trademark.

The use in this publication of trade names, trademarks, service marks, and similar terms, even if they are not identified as such, is not to be taken as an expression of opinion as to whether or not they are subject to proprietary rights.

While the advice and information in this book are believed to be true and accurate at the date of publication, neither the authors nor the editors nor the publisher can accept any legal responsibility for any errors or omissions that may be made. The publisher makes no warranty, express or implied, with respect to the material contained herein.

Managing Director, Apress Media LLC: Welmoed Spahr
Acquisitions Editor: Jonathan Gennick
Development Editor: Laura Berendson
Coordinating Editor: Jill Balzano

Cover image designed by Freepik (www.freepik.com)

Distributed to the book trade worldwide by Springer Science+Business Media New York, 233 Spring Street, 6th Floor, New York, NY 10013. Phone 1-800-SPRINGER, fax (201) 348-4505, e-mail orders-ny@springer-sbm.com, or visit www.springeronline.com. Apress Media, LLC is a California LLC and the sole member (owner) is Springer Science + Business Media Finance Inc (SSBM Finance Inc). SSBM Finance Inc is a **Delaware** corporation.

For information on translations, please e-mail booktranslations@springernature.com; for reprint, paperback, or audio rights, please e-mail bookpermissions@springernature.com.

Apress titles may be purchased in bulk for academic, corporate, or promotional use. eBook versions and licenses are also available for most titles. For more information, reference our Print and eBook Bulk Sales web page at http://www.apress.com/bulk-sales.

Any source code or other supplementary material referenced by the author in this book is available to readers on GitHub via the book's product page, located at www.apress.com/9781484258163. For more detailed information, please visit http://www.apress.com/source-code.

Printed on acid-free paper

I dedicate this book to my father David who was a pioneer in relational databases and founder of Rctck. He inspired me to build and experiment and encouraged me to pursue a career in information technology and databases.

Table of Contents

About the Author

Nicholas Cottrell has used MongoDB for many software development projects since version 2.0 long before joining the company in 2017. He worked as a consulting engineer, delivering training and helping enterprise customers optimize and scale their big data projects. He transitioned to a technical services role in late 2018, helping customers triage critical problems with their MongoDB deployments. Nic gives regular talks, including at MongoDB local events and at MongoDB World in NYC. He holds dual Australian and Swedish citizenship and lives in Normandy, France.

About the Technical Reviewer

Stephen Steneker is Director of Developer Engagement at MongoDB. He is a specialist software generalist who enjoys a steady diet of open source, data, database, wordplay, and dad humor.

Acknowledgments

I need to send a special thanks to my wife Sophie, daughter Lucie, and son James for their constant support and unending patience during the evenings and weekends while I wrote this book.

I also wish to thank my colleagues Wes, Idan, and Clare for additional proofreading and feedback and to all my fellow engineers at MongoDB for creating such amazing products.

CHAPTER 1

Core Concepts

For those coming from the world of traditional relational database management systems or even enterprise-level Microsoft SQL Server or Oracle, MongoDB presents an innovative way of thinking about scaling and availability. This chapter introduces all the core concepts of MongoDB deployments and explains how MongoDB nodes achieve high-availability, low-latency replication, and handle unexpected infrastructure failures.

> *Redundancy is ambiguous because it seems like a waste if nothing unusual happens. Except that something unusual happens-usually.*
>
> —Nassim Nicholas Taleb, scholar, risk analyst, and author of *The Black Swan*

Key features of MongoDB

Storing structured data has been an issue since the dawn of the computer age. Initially kept in delimited files, eventually stored in predefined data tables, but more recently a new age of databases has appeared which record data in key/value stores, graphs, and complex multilevel documents. None of these relative newcomers is any less "relational" than the old SQL solutions. MongoDB allows developers to represent relationships, but in a much more intuitive and flexible way with *structured documents*.

The other advantage of MongoDB is that it is built to be efficient, scalable, and redundant at its core. By running on commodity hardware, enterprises can build powerful "Big Data" solutions on their own data centers and easily scale them up as the application grows and evolves.

Now that high-capacity, low-latency storage is relatively cheap, the entire paradigm of database design has changed. SQL database design focused on keeping databases as small as possible using *normalization,* but this could have huge costs at read time when

1

© Nicholas Cottrell 2020
N. Cottrell, *MongoDB Topology Design*, https://doi.org/10.1007/978-1-4842-5817-0_1

it was necessary to *join* data back together into logical blocks. By storing related data together in a single document, more disk space may be required, but read performance is extremely optimized with no need for any "joins" or other processing at read time.

MongoDB has been designed for high availability with its distributed architecture while still maintaining durable and consistent changes. In production deployments, there will be multiple MongoDB *nodes* each with a complete copy of the data that is kept in sync via *replication*. MongoDB uses a variation of the master/slave paradigm in that one member of a *replica set* is designated the *primary* and is responsible for acknowledging any write operations, and the others are *secondaries* and maintain a copy of the data. These secondaries are a sort of *disaster recovery* standby and will take over the role of primary should it become unavailable. Architecture choices will be discussed in detail in future chapters on topologies and sharding.

Differences to "traditional databases"

Traditional databases like Oracle, MySQL, or Microsoft SQL Server use a tabular paradigm for storing data – much like a spreadsheet. They require system architects or developers to decompose logical objects of data into multiple tables requiring both additional complexity for software development and also additional I/O when writing changes to many different locations on the storage device.

Terminology

While many concepts like queries, indexes, and transactions are very similar, Table 1-1 presents the key terminology and differences between traditional SQL databases and MongoDB.

Table 1-1. *A comparison between common SQL and MongoDB terms*

SQL	MongoDB	Notes
Table	Collection	Contains documents sharing a similar entity type, but not necessarily the exact same set of fields.
Row	Document	An entity with a unique ID field and other data fields.
Column	Field	Not all documents must have the same fields. Fields can be added to individual documents without rebuilding any data files. Fields can have many data types, including nested arrays of subdocuments.
Index	Index	MongoDB also supports secondary, partial, sparse, geospatial, case-insensitive, and compound indexes.
Query	Query	MongoDB queries are defined as documents.
View	View	MongoDB supports read-only views and in MongoDB 4.2+ also on-demand materialized views.
Transaction	Transaction	MongoDB 4.2+ supports multidocument transactions in sharded deployments.
Master/slave	Primary/secondary	Unlike many systems, the role of primary and secondary is fluid and react automatically during maintenance and network failures.
Replication	Replication	MongoDB uses logical operation logs rather than copying binary data deltas.
	Deployment	Any group of MongoDB nodes working together in a particular configuration.
	Cluster	A MongoDB deployment with one or more shards, config servers, and routers.
	Shard	A set of MongoDB nodes which contain a subset of data.

Storage engines

Like many other popular databases, MongoDB has support for alternative storage engines. This was particularly important during the transition from the original memory-mapped storage solution (now called `MMAPv1`) to the new WiredTiger storage engine which became the default in version 3.2. WiredTiger offers superior concurrency features as well as compression, encryption, and other internal functions now required for modern MongoDB functionality.

Binary JSON

While we interact with MongoDB via JSON documents for queries, administrative commands, and configuration, the database server itself actually manipulates a special binary-encoded format of JSON called BSON ("Binary JSON"). This format defines a number of data types not available in standard JSON such as `Decimal128` (a 128-bit precision decimal) and `Date` (a 64-bit UTC timestamp). An Extended JSON format is also available to support expressions like `{"$numberDecimal":"10.99"}` and `{"$date":"2019-08-11T17:54:14.692Z"}` for exporting data into human-readable format.

BSON also has the benefit of being lightweight, traversable, and efficient. The format is very simple and the format specification is open source. It has little overhead and so minimizes bytes needed to be transferred or stored. The format reserves some bytes to indicate subdocument sizes, making it algorithmically efficient to walk complex documents and skip to target fields. Finally, its format is easily decoded, encoded, and compressed.

Data files

Every collection and index requires a WiredTiger file on disk. Most operating systems set an upper limit on the maximum number resources available (files, threads, memory, etc.) by a single process. Very large deployments with many collections, indexes, or active connections can sometimes hit these limits. One common cause is a *multi-tenant pattern* discussed later in this chapter.

Note   In Unix-type operating systems, file descriptors are used for almost any operations that read or write, I/O devices, pipes, and network sockets; no many open network connections can also exhaust this limit.

Concurrency

Like any database which supports high levels of concurrency from many clients writing and querying data in parallel, MongoDB uses a multiversion concurrency control (MVCC) system which uses *snapshot isolation* to implement optimistic concurrency control. Few operations require global locks and most lock at the document level. However, some administrative commands (such as `compact`) can still lock an entire logical database for extended periods, so these should be run in a rolling manner to avoid downtime. Some commands (such as `createIndex`) will lock at the collection level, forcing all changes to documents in that collection to be queued.

Relationships

Let's imagine that we are building a national library platform and we have three large collections of documents: (1) books, (2) borrowers, and (3) authors.

In Figure 1-1, we see both the structured and relational nature of MongoDB documents. In **Author** documents, there is a field `books`, with three subfields `id`, `title`, and `cover_img`. This lets us reference a **Book** document in another collection by `id` but also keeps the title locally since it's not going to change. If we want to render the Author's bio on the website, this document already has all the required values, and so a second round-trip to the database can be avoided.

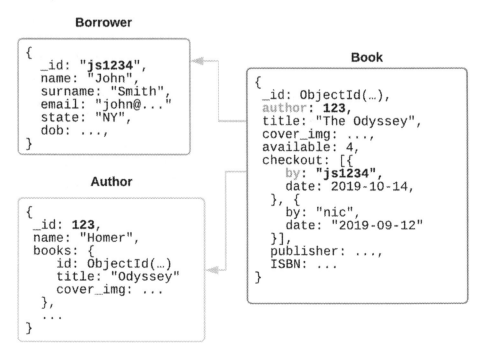

Figure 1-1. *Example documents for our collections*

We see a similar pattern in the **Book** document. The checkout array contains multiple entries for each borrower who currently has a copy checked out. We represent them as an array of subdocuments, with by and date fields. The by value references the **Borrower** document's unique _id field. The **Book** document contains all the data required to see both how many copies remain in the library system and who has checked out books right now.

In an **SQL database**, we would need a separate borrower_history table to represent the many-to-many relationship between borrowers and books.

Referential integrity

Maintaining valid relationships within a database such as the concept of using *secondary keys* in SQL databases is known as *referential integrity*. Once again, the one-to-many mapping of SQL tables is normally represented in a single document in MongoDB, and so the problem of maintaining integrity across multiple tables is almost completely avoided. Of course, it is sometimes necessary to express and store more complex relationships in MongoDB, and software architects and developers need to consider how to keep such relationships consistent in the database.

While there is no such thing as a *foreign key constraint* nor *cascading deletes* in MongoDB, most design patterns and *object-data mappers* (ODMs) make it easy for the application to maintain these references.

In our earlier library example in SQL, if I wanted to delete a person from a borrower table, the database would need to delete every entry from a borrower_history table. But we would be deleting valuable historical information.

In the age of cheap storage, the paradigm has shifted, and we want to keep as much data as possible. Rather than actually deleting the borrower document, in MongoDB we would rather mark the person as inactive by setting a field active to false. Since we are keeping all the borrower history, the problem of foreign key constraint violations is avoided too.

In most cases, it's up to the application to use a multidocument transaction to update both sides of the relationship. In reality this is a much better way to code and create application logic, since it keeps everything inside the application codebase, rather than having some constraint and validation performed on the database side and some on the application side.

With data protection regulations and the "right to be forgotten" in the European Union's General Data Protection Regulation and other similar regulations, it is sometimes necessary to delete user's data completely. This is discussed in Chapter 4.

ACID compliance

ACID stands for *atomicity, consistency, isolation,* and *durability.* These four characteristics of traditional databases were considered to be the cornerstone of any production-ready system and were often used as an argument against MongoDB. Historically MongoDB has always provided a flexible approach which allows application developers to choose the level of durability and consistency they require and lets them balance speed, throughput, and cost.

Atomicity

Atomicity refers to the ability to perform an "all or nothing" transaction of multiple changes inside the database. If one part of the change is not possible (e.g., due to violating a unique constraint), then the whole transaction should fail. This was particularly important within "relational databases" which used separate tables of data to represent one-to-many relationships.

In MongoDB, most such relationships are recorded inside a single document, and document-level atomicity has been a core feature of MongoDB since the earliest versions. For example, in Listing 1-1 we see an example which first checks the availability of a book and only then performs a checkout. If two threads both tried to check out the last copy of the book simultaneously, only one thread would succeed. Furthermore, by being atomic at the document level, an update to a document will change all field values, or none at all.

Listing 1-1. An example of document-level atomicity "checking out a book"

```
db.books.findAndModify ( {
   query: {
           _id: 123456789,
           available: { $gt: 0 }
         },
   update: {
             $inc: { available: -1 },
             $push: { checkout:
                { by: " nic", date: new Date() } }
           }
} )
```

MongoDB 4.0 introduced full transactions against multiple documents in different collections as long as the collection was not sharded. In MongoDB 4.2 complex transactions that included sharded collections are also supported, matching the abilities of any SQL database, although probably only needed for a small subset of use cases.

Consistency

This property is about keeping the data in a valid state and free from corruption. Since MongoDB uses MVCC to control consistency of data at the document level, an update to a document that changes several fields will either completely succeed or fail. Failures can be caused by situations like a *unique key constraint* or *schema validation* violation. Internally, MVCC implements a snapshot isolation guarantee which ensures that each operation always sees a consistent snapshot of data. Since MongoDB 3.6, causally consistent sessions can be used to execute causal operations in a particular order, as long as majority writes and reads are employed. MongoDB 4.2 added support for multidocument transactions in sharded collections, making it possible to ensure relational integrity in critical and complex operations such as financial transactions.

Isolation

Read isolation is a difficult concept in any database and particularly in distributed databases where some application processes are explicitly choosing to read from secondary members who may be lagging behind the primary. The application can specify a `local` read concern for a particular query (much like an *isolation level*) to choose to read data before it has been made fully durable throughout the entire distributed set. This allows for faster, less complex read operations, but the application may risk reading data that may be later rolled back.

In most cases, the application should read from the primary to ensure that it gets the latest data. Although, using *read concern majority* will ensure that only data that is fully durable will be returned. This incurs some additional processing and latency penalties. See corresponding details about *majority writes* in Chapter 5.

In MongoDB, explicit *transactions* should only be used in critical code paths where several related documents must be updated together atomically. In this case, isolation works much the same as in any database. Any writes that are made inside the transaction are not visible to any other query until the transaction is committed.

For example, if you are processing a financial transaction which affects multiple documents in the same or a different collection, then a transaction may be appropriate with an explicit `start` and `commit`/`abort` step.

Note   When transactions abort, all changes made in the transaction are completely discarded without ever being visible to any other process outside the transaction.

Fully *distributed transactions* (affecting sharded collections) incur an additional cost in terms of processing power and latency to an operation and should only be used when absolutely necessary. If you are making several unrelated changes together, then you should not use transactions at all.

Bulk operations

For additional performance, MongoDB supports bulk operations which can be sent over the wire together and processed more efficiently by the server. The application can choose to make these bulk operations *ordered* or not. When ordered, any error will cancel subsequent operations in the queue. When unordered, the server will try and process all operations even if some of them fail. In both cases, the application is told which operations failed and why. This allows for flexible error handling and retries if deemed appropriate in the business logic. When run outside a transaction, bulk operations are atomic and isolated at the document level only.

Note   In order to avoid the particular situation where two processes might simultaneously try to insert a value for the first time, you should configure a *unique index* on that field. This will prevent duplicate data, and one of the processes will receive a unique index violation when it inserts, which can be handled by the application.

Durability

In the ACID paradigm, durability means that a write operation has been committed to a point where a sudden crash of the server will not lose that operation.

Journal and flushing

MongoDB uses a familiar *write-ahead journal* file to help ensure that writes are made durable as soon as possible. When a client sends a write operation to a node, it is first applied in memory, then written to the journal on disk, and then approximately every 60 seconds all changes queued in memory (including indexes) are flushed to disk creating a durable *checkpoint*.

By queuing changes in memory first, MongoDB can achieve much higher throughput since it can discard any obsolete changes (e.g., when the same document's field is changed twice within 60 seconds) and then batch all remaining I/O operations together.

For a *standalone* MongoDB node, we can consider a write durable once it has been written to the journal, which should occur at least every 50 milliseconds. As part of the mongod startup process, it will check the journal and apply any operations that were written ahead there during a previous session.

For *replica sets*, we can consider a write durable only once it has been written to a majority of nodes. At this point, if the primary's storage suddenly fails entirely, a secondary with this write would become the primary and the change could never be lost.

Scaling

While traditional databases have added implementations of distribution and replication, MongoDB provides a simple yet extremely flexible pair of features called *replication* and *sharding* to create deployments that can be tailored to match the availability, performance, and cost requirements of almost any project.

In MongoDB, replication means that logical operations are replicated between all the data-bearing nodes in a *replica set* (see Figure 1-2). Rather than sending a binary version of the change delta, the change operation is recorded in an idempotent log of operations (called the *oplog*), and these same operations are replicated and applied in the on secondaries as they are on the primary. By avoiding *binary replication*, MongoDB will not replicate any filesystem-based errors that may be introduced by a faulty storage device.

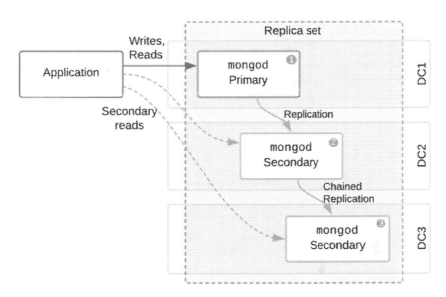

Figure 1-2. _A replica set with three data-bearing nodes_

In some legacy topologies, an arbiter was deployed in a third data center to arbitrate during network partitions. It is now strongly recommended to avoid arbiters and instead deploy only data-bearing nodes.

For larger deployments, MongoDB introduces the concept of _sharding_ as illustrated in Figure 1-3. Each _shard_ is comprised of a replica set (to provide redundancy) and stores a subset of the entire data for sharded collections. This could be considered a sort of "multi-master" deployment where each primary is responsible for a certain range of documents. For these _sharded clusters,_ we also need to introduce a mongos router which hides the complexity from the application. This mongos functions separately from the shards and their components and will redirect any incoming write operations to whichever replica set member is currently the primary.

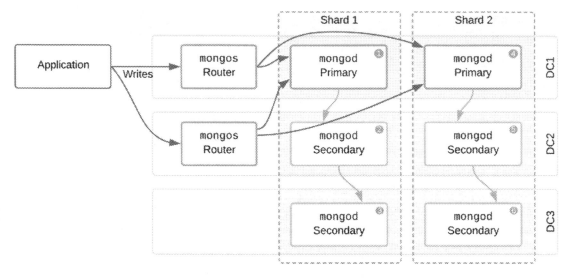

Figure 1-3. *A sharded cluster with two shards (each being a replica set)*

From the perspective of the application, a `mongos` router node behaves almost identically to any other node. Moving from a replica set topology to a sharded cluster only requires an application to update the connection URI to point to the `mongos` routers rather than the member nodes directly.

Replication

Now that we have introduced the concept of replication, let's dive deeper into some of the internal mechanisms so that we see how they might be affected by our topology design.

Syncing

There are two main stages for syncing a node in a replica set:

1. An *initial sync* where all of the data is copied over the network and the data and indexes are rebuilt from scratch on the target node

2. Incremental oplog processing where a *batch of updates* already performed on the primary is applied to the data on a secondary

An initial sync is a resource-intensive process as both network and storage capacity can be bottlenecks. This should only happen when

(i)   A new node is added to an existing replica set

(ii) A node has been offline so long that it cannot catch up based on the oplog available or

(iii) Storage-level corruption means that the existing data files can no longer be trusted

Elections

MongoDB decides which node in a replica set becomes the primary by holding an election. System architects can set priorities for certain nodes, but in general the node that has the most recent writes is elected primary to minimize data loss in worst-case scenarios. With proper use of majority write concern, writes can be guaranteed to never be lost from network failures. This will be discussed further in Chapter 5.

Lag/staleness

Because nodes normally reside on different hosts (and preferably also in different data centers), there will always be some delay in replication as the oplog data streams over the network to each secondary. Each secondary will apply the same oplog changes as fast as possible. The time between when a write is completed on the primary and when the secondary applies that same change is called the *replication lag*. Secondaries can pull oplog updates from either the primary or another secondary via *replication chaining*.

When the application writes with *majority*, it must wait for a majority of data-bearing nodes to write before moving on to the next operation. As a consequence of waiting, replication lag *decreases* but *throughput* will also be lower.

An application can choose to write certain changes without an explicit write concern. In this mode by default, a write concern value of 1 is used, and the application will wait only for the primary to acknowledge the change but not for any secondaries. Should the primary then fail, the write may never get replicated. These writes would eventually be *rolled back* when the node later rejoins the replica set and will then be written to a special local `rollback` file on disk. Manual intervention is then required to reintegrate these rolled back writes into the database.

Only certain cases when throughput is more important than durability (such as hit logs or "Internet of Things" metrics) should consider {w: 1} writes in production.

Oplog window

By default, each replica set member creates the oplog as a capped collection with a fixed size between about 1GB and 50GB depending on the amount of free disk space available on the data volume at the time. It's also possible to increase the size of the oplog collection later, if this initial size proves insufficient.

The *oplog window* is the number of *hours* of most recent changes kept in the oplog, calculated from the difference in timestamps between the oldest and most recent oplog entry. This window will change over time as it is dependent on how heavy the workload and how compact the update operations are.

All nodes in a replica set should be configured with an oplog size sufficient for at least 72 hours under normal loads to allow for fast recovery and SLAs to be met even over a weekend.

Read preference

We introduced the concept of customizable isolation levels when reading data from replica sets. Remember that secondary nodes may lag behind the primary, and by reading from anything but a primary, we risk reading stale data. In cases where this is acceptable, the application can choose to read from other nodes based on different performance and latency metrics outlined in Table 1-2.

Table 1-2. *Custom read preferences to balance application priorities*

Goal	Method
Maximize consistency	Use `primary` read preference and `majority` read concern to only see writes that will never be rolled back.
Maximize availability	Use `primaryPreferred` to get consistent reads when there's a primary and stale reads when only secondaries are available.
Minimize latency	Use `nearest` to get fast read responses, but with possible *stale* results.
Target workloads	Use `secondaryPreferred` with tags to avoid pressure on the primary, and control which secondaries are used.
Protect primary	Use `secondary` for special high-impact workloads (such as aggregations with no index) so that the primary will *never* be overloaded.

We will explore some real-world usages of these read preferences more in Chapter 5.

States

Due to the distributed nature of a replica set, each node can be in any number of states which will affect its own behavior and how applications (and their drivers) can interact with that node. We have already mentioned the common roles which correspond to states such as PRIMARY, SECONDARY, and ARBITER.

It's important to understand the other possible states because they can affect the behavior of your deployment during disaster recovery efforts when it's critical to keep the application operational and able to continue writing changes durably.

Table 1-3. *Description of the possible member states*

State	Notes	Can vote?
STARTUP	The initial state of mongod as it reads its config and loads necessary data into memory.	Yes
PRIMARY	The node is online, has won an election, and is accepting writes from client.	
SECONDARY	The node is online and is replicating from the primary. It may have a delayed copy of the data.	
RECOVERING	The node has joined the replica set but is not ready to accept reads, as it is currently performing some administrative functions.	
STARTUP2	The node has actively joined the set, but is currently copying data from another member via an initial sync.	
ROLLBACK	The node was formerly the primary, but was disconnected from the set. It is online but is *rolling back changes*, so that it can catch up to the current primary.	
ARBITER	This node maintains connections to facilitate health checks and elections.	
DOWN	This node once communicated with the set, but stopped communicating and is likely offline or partitioned from the rest of the network.	No
UNKNOWN	This member has never communicated its state to the others.	
REMOVED	This member was removed from the set and will no longer replicate data.	

Figure 1-4 maps the most common transitions between the different states.

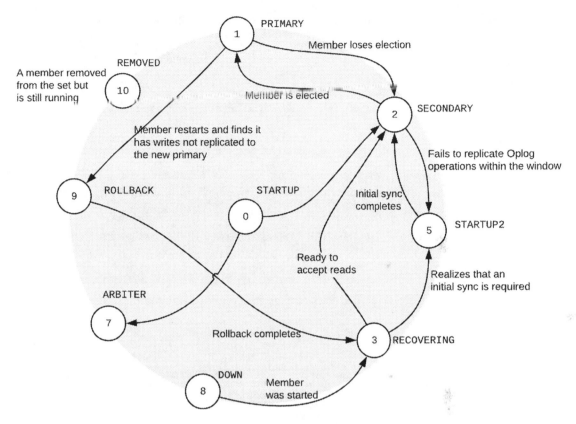

Figure 1-4. *Common transitions between states*

Sharding

In order to scale out writes, sharding the data into subsets each with their own primary node is a way of creating a form of "master-master" topology available in some legacy databases.

In MongoDB, sharding is a design decision that should be taken in agreement between developers and database administrators.

When it's time to shard these collections, we have to choose a *shard key* to partition the data. This shard key must be selective and should form part of common queries so that the mongos router can *target* an exact shard. For example, if we shard our book collection by {author: 1, _id: 1} and we do a query for {author: 123}, then normally all matching documents will exist on a single shard. We want to avoid *scatter-gather queries* which require querying all shards in the cluster and then merging results on the router since this approach **does not scale** efficiently.

Once a *shard key* has been chosen and a collection has been sharded, it requires manual intervention to change the shard key since the data has now been distributed across the cluster. This will be discussed further in Chapters 10 and 11.

Chunks

In order to manage sharding for collections which may have billions or trillions of documents, it is necessary to group documents into logical *chunks*. Each chunk is defined as a range of values based on the chosen shard key fields. In Figure 1-5, we see an example collection with four documents sharded with a *simple shard key* on field customer. Chunk 1 contains all documents with customer values from effectively negative infinity up to but not including 5. Chunk 2 has documents with customer value 5 and higher.

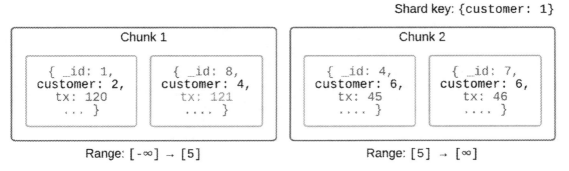

Figure 1-5. Documents grouped in chunk ranges

As the number of documents increases over time, it may become necessary to split up Chunk 1 into two, as seen in Figure 1-6. Note that *New Chunk 1A*'s lower boundary and that *New Chunk 1B*'s upper boundary are the same as their parent *Chunk 1*. This splitting step requires updating some metadata on the config database and has relatively low impact. Migration is a separate subsequent step.

Figure 1-6. *Two chunks newly split from an original chunk*

As we have created a shard key on just `customer`, the smallest range would be a single customer ID value. Documents for this customer could never be distributed over more than one chunk, making it harder to balance this cluster.

Note   In reality, MongoDB uses `MinKey` and `MaxKey` rather than negative infinity to infinity to identify chunk boundaries since the values may be of any BSON data type and not just integers.

Choice of shard key

A good shard key is critical to maximize sharded performance over time and future-proof deployments as more shards are added. It must

1.   Have high cardinality to ensure chunks can be split into smaller chunks as the data grows

2.   Be present in most queries so that the `mongos` can target specific shards

3.   Distribute writes randomly (and thus evenly) across all shards

4.   Avoid fields with monotonically increasing values

In Figure 1-7 we see a single shard key on the field `productId` which can be a good shard key for a massive ecommerce site and will distribute evenly as long as values are not monotonically increasing. In reality, most good shard keys are *compound* with two or more fields, the first for targeting and the second to ensure high cardinality.

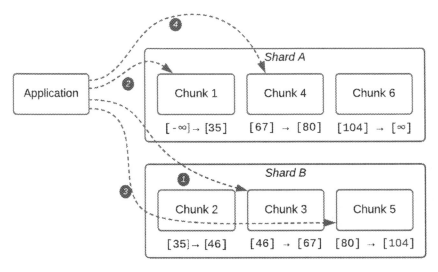

Shard key: {productId: 1}

Figure 1-7. *Writes distributed evenly across shards*

Hashed shard keys can also be defined on a single field. Based on a corresponding hashed index, this type of shard key can distribute documents evenly over a wider chunk range.

Balancer

A balancer process works to balance the number of *chunks* evenly among the shards. Depending on how the chunk boundaries are drawn, some chunks may contain more documents than others. So even if the number of documents per chunk is equal, some documents may be bigger than others leading to slightly different data size per chunk.

Shard distribution

You can run db.<collection>.getShardDistribution() on each sharded collection to see metadata about distribution. Listing 1-2 shows a balanced cluster with two shards. The balancer tries to ensure the number of chunks is the same on each shard, but depending on insertion patterns, the number of documents in a chunk and the average size of documents may mean that the size of data between chunks can sometimes vary significantly.

Listing 1-2. Sharding metadata showing a balanced sharded cluster

```
Shard prod-a at prod-a/node-a1.local:27018,node-a2.local: 27018,
node-a3.local: 27018
data : 512.34Mb docs : 76861 chunks : 26
estimated data per chunk : 19.71Mb
estimated docs per chunk : 2956

Shard prod-b at prod-b/node-b1.local:27018,node-b2.local:27018,
node-b3.local:27018
data : 456.78Mb docs : 79142 chunks : 27
estimated data per chunk : 16.92Mb
estimated docs per chunk : 2931

Totals
data : 969.12Mb docs : 156003 chunks : 53
Shard prod-a contains 52.8% data, 49.3% docs in cluster, avg obj size on
shard : 267b
Shard prod-b contains 47.2% data, 50.7% docs in cluster, avg obj size on
shard : 224b
```

Pre-splitting

When restoring or importing a large amount of data into an empty sharded collection, it is much more efficient to *pre-split chunks* if you already know approximately how the values will be distributed. This means that the mongorestore via the mongos will immediately distribute document inserts directly across shards. With a well-defined pre-split, the chunks should be equally distributed, and there shouldn't be much for the balancer to redistribute over the network after restoring data.

The command in Listing 1-3 will create 16,384 equally sized chunks across all the current shards and will give almost perfectly even distribution of new document inserts.

Listing 1-3. Command to pre-split with a hashed shard key

```
db.adminCommand({
  shardCollection: "cacheDB.userCache",
  key: { _id: 'hashed' },
  numInitialChunks: 16384
})
```

Ascending shard keys and hot shards

Let's imagine a slight variation on our first chunk example where the collection stores documents about the user account and the shard key includes a version field v which is usually between 1 and 3 and therefore has low cardinality.

When new users sign up to this service, they are assigned a *monotonically increasing* customer ID number custId. In the example shown in Figure 1-8, we see the next customers to sign up will get IDs 9433, 9434, and 9435. All of these will naturally fall into *Chunk 1000*'s range and will be routed to Shard B. In fact, any of the most recent half of our customers will be routed to Shard B for both reads and writes, while the oldest (and possibly less active ones) will be routed to Shard A. In this scenario we consider Shard B to be a *hot shard* as it is receiving a clear majority of the cluster's workload. This scaling design fails even when adding more shards as the chunk with range ending in infinity will receive *all* the insert operations.

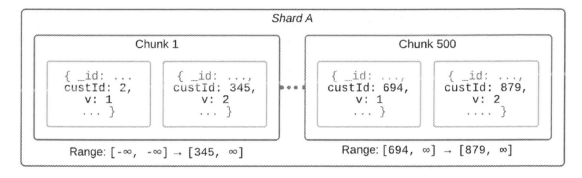

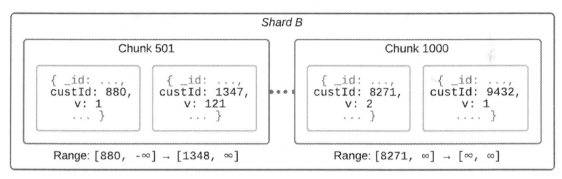

Shard key: {custId: 1, v: 1}

Figure 1-8. *A sharded cluster with a hot shard taking all new inserts*

There are several alternatives which will be discussed in Chapters 10 and 11 on advanced sharding techniques.

Architecture choices

Now that we understand the major concepts of MongoDB replication and sharding, it's time to consider how to best lay out the underlying infrastructure to most efficiently and cost-effectively host our deployment in a scalable and performant manner.

In many cases when we are facing challenges in maximizing performance of a cluster, it's good to think in terms of bottlenecks. The usual bottlenecks are *CPU* processing, available *memory*, *storage I/O* capacity, and *network* latency, bandwidth, or congestion.

Computing resources

MongoDB has been designed to run on commodity hardware and doesn't require any special expensive enterprise-ready hardware. Having said that, there are a number of hardware choices for any hosts (virtual or otherwise) which can create a good baseline performance.

Memory

Firstly, the nodes should have sufficient memory to keep a *working set* of documents and indexes in memory. By avoiding a round-trip to the storage device, MongoDB is able to service incoming requests and changes extremely quickly. This working set is hard to predict in advance, since it represents the documents that are actively being accessed and changed in a given period. Simulating workloads with real data is the best way to gauge the working set requirements of your application.

When a request comes in to change a document, or execute a query, if the data is already in the WiredTiger storage engine's memory cache, then there is no need to wait for slower storage-layer lookups. Even writes can be performed purely in memory in a concurrent manner and will be flushed to disk every 60 seconds or so.

In the evolution of any application, as load increases, at some point the working set will expand past the physical memory available to the host, and suddenly I/O will become a bottleneck as the cache of document in memory "churns" and changes written in memory need to be flushed to disk early. It is important to monitor real memory growth and swap usage during peak times to detect these limits early and react by increasing memory resources, or sharding.

Storage

At the current price per gigabyte, solid-state storage (SSD) should be the bare minimum for any new deployment infrastructure. Spinning hard drives (HDD) should be avoided at all costs due to the extremely high seek latency which will slow down random reads.

Most cloud providers offer multiple levels of storage device latency. The *provisioned* input/output operations per second (IOPS) storage often provides much lower latency for a reasonable additional cost.

Another way to further reduce storage latency and improve throughput is to use the newer NVMe (Nonvolatile Memory Express) technology. Some cloud providers even offer local NVMe storage on certain classes of virtual machine instances. Note, however, that often these are offered as ephemeral drives and *all data may be lost* should the instance ever be stopped (either explicitly or due to data center failures). Therefore, be careful to have at least one node running on persistent storage to avoid complete data loss should all instances be shut down simultaneously,

Bandwidth and latency

Designing for low latency will be crucial in achieving a high-performance distributed database. There are many different hardware options available, and manufacturers are working hard to reduce latency and increase bandwidth at each level and with each new iteration.

As we can see in Table 1-4, memory is still much faster than persistent storage technologies, but some of the most recent SSD storage devices can now compete in terms of bandwidth with older memory technologies.

Table 1-4. *Access speeds of different storage (approximate)*

Category	Seek Latency	Read Bandwidth (Sequential)
L1 Cache	2 ns (2–3 clock cycles)	~3500MB/s
L2 Cache	5 ns (~10 clock cycles)	~4000MB/s
Memory (DDR4)	70 ns	~3000MB/s
Memory (DDR3)	80 ns	~2000MB/s
SDD with Nonvolatile Memory Express (NVMe)	120,000 ns (0.1 ms)	~2500MB/s (with 4 lanes)
SSD Storage (SATA 3.0)	500,000 ns (0.5 ms)	~550MB/s
HDD Storage (SAS/FC)	12×10^6 ns (13 ms)	~200MB/s
SAN (Fiber Channel, iSCSI) Network Storage	Storage latency + additional 200–700 ns	200MB/s–16GB/s

We can conclude that investing in the right SSD and memory technologies can easily double the I/O performance of your database nodes.

Even though the read bandwidth of memory is no longer much higher than SSD storage, the latency is about 1000 times lower. In most cases, queries will first read an index, then load and return a small document (a few hundred bytes in size) and so the latency is much more important to performance than bandwidth.

Note   Memory performance actually drops with increasing size. The latency of 8GB sticks is about 50% slower than 4GB. The cost per GB does not scale favorably either.

Horizontal scaling

Once you have exhausted the vertical scaling possibilities for your nodes and your replica set is not able to service all the write requests from the application (or the data size on disk has exceeded about 2TB), then it's time to scale *horizontally* with sharding.

Note   The 2TB recommended limit for shard size is based on practical limitations of storage and network throughput in order to allow initial syncs and restores to complete within an acceptable time span.

With sharding, we can spread the load across multiple primary nodes and from that point on can increase capacity further by adding additional shards as the workload or data increases. This can be the most cost-effective way to increase overall memory resources and total cluster performance.

Round-trip latency

In MongoDB, like any distributed system, one bottleneck can be the time taken to send a packet of data between the components and get a response back. Known as round-trip time (RTT) latency, this affects how many of the components of a MongoDB cluster chose to route requests.

This latency is usually recorded in milliseconds, and is bounded by a number of factors. The physical distance between any pair of hosts (and the speed of light), the congestion of the network, the chosen route through the network (number of hops), and delays added by switches along the way are common factors which can add to latency.

If possible, a direct dedicated fiber connection between data centers should be used to reduce this as much as possible.

In a sharded cluster, the application queries via a mongos router node, and so there are two different sets of round-trips as shown in Figure 1-9. In this example, we see that Application$_1$ has lower latency to the mongos nodes in the same data center. Based on this, the driver in Application$_1$ will distribute its queries via mongos$_1$ and mongos$_2$, whereas Application$_2$ will route all queries to mongos$_3$ in DC2. However, if mongos$_3$ fails, Application$_2$ will automatically and instantly failover to the mongos available in DC1 since they now represent the best possible RTTs.

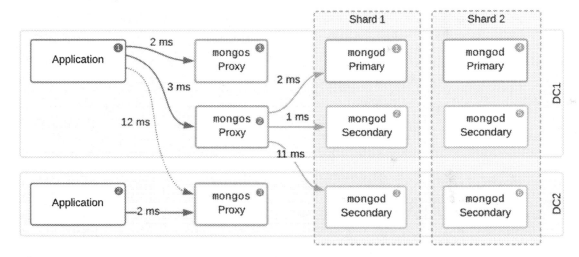

Figure 1-9. *Latencies between components in a 2-DC deployment*

The second pair of round-trips is between the mongos instances and the data-bearing nodes in the shard. By default, reads and writes will go via the primary. However, if the application requests nearest read preference, then queries would be sent to either mongod$_1$ or mongod$_2$ since they have the lowest RTTs at 2ms and 1ms, respectively.

Private vs. cloud

The rest of this book will focus on cases where customers want to build high-performance, highly available self-managed MongoDB deployments. Until recently most production MongoDB deployments were deployed on companies' own data centers – so-called "*on-prem*" deployments.

Many large corporations now find that the major cloud providers like AWS, Azure, and GCP are sufficiently stable and cost-effective that they can run virtual machines on the cloud as "*self-managed cloud*" servers. We will sometimes compare what is possible on-prem to MongoDB's own *fully managed* solution called MongoDB Atlas.

Logical databases

Like most database management systems, MongoDB allows for multiple *logical databases* to exist on a single physical deployment. Each logical database can have its own collections of data and its own users with custom roles and privileges. The data files of these databases are still in the same path, however, so taking *LVM* (Logical Volume Manager) backups of the storage volumes will necessarily back up all logical databases together.

In the so-called "*multi-tenant*" setups, a single physical MongoDB deployment will often have many databases each for a separate customer. For certain *SaaS* (software as a service) offerings, each database will have a number of almost identical smaller collections each having matching the same schema.

Key takeaways

From this chapter, the key concepts to remember are as follows:

- MongoDB databases store structured documents with a range of data types using a special binary JSON-like format called BSON.

- MongoDB deployments can be standalone nodes, replica set, or sharded clusters where data is broken into subsets for scaling out for humongous datasets.

- MongoDB databases support ACID compliance even for multidocument transactions on sharded clusters.

- The replication mechanism is robust and asynchronous, handling automatic failover.

- Writes and reads can be tuned for performance over consistency if desired.

- Sharded collections are distributed based on a user-defined shard key and migrated in chunks to keep the shards balanced.

- MongoDB deployments can be automated on-prem or in self-managed cloud infrastructure.

- A fully managed MongoDB service called Atlas is also available to avoid managing any infrastructure directly.

CHAPTER 2

Fault-Tolerant Design

This chapter delves deeper into the fault-tolerant nature of MongoDB and explores some of the special types of nodes and how they should be used on production systems. We look at common errors that may occur in real-world systems and how to mitigate them.

Redundancy is expensive but indispensable.

—Jane Jacobs, urbanist, writer, and activist

Special nodes

We have already covered the standard types of nodes in a MongoDB deployment. These data-bearing nodes keep a complete copy of the data via the replication mechanism and can become a primary node at any time should the current primary fail for any reason. Next, we will discuss some other types of nodes that can be used in certain special cases.

In the early days of MongoDB before robust production-ready backup solutions were available and when reliable SSD storage was particularly expensive, some of the following types of nodes had a justifiable place in production configurations. However, with the advent of cheaper hardware and more advanced features such as majority write concern, some of the following nodes should now be avoided in production deployments. We will cover the historical use cases and the current alternative best practices.

Arbiters

Arbiters are a type of MongoDB node that join a replica set with the sole role of participating in elections. They do not store any user data, but will only maintain a copy of the replica set metadata in order to know which members they should connect to and how to communicate securely.

31

© Nicholas Cottrell 2020
N. Cottrell, *MongoDB Topology Design*, https://doi.org/10.1007/978-1-4842-5817-0_2

These are one of the few "exotic" node types that are still regularly used in production deployments, but only really required when less than three distinct data centers are available. This will be discussed further in Chapters 5 and 6 on *basic* and *global topologies*. Some customers with two data centers will place a single arbiter in a cloud instance since their data protection policies do not allow user data to be stored in the cloud.

In Figure 2-1 we see that replication occurs between data centers 1 and 2, but only health "pings" are communicated with the arbiter node residing in the cloud.

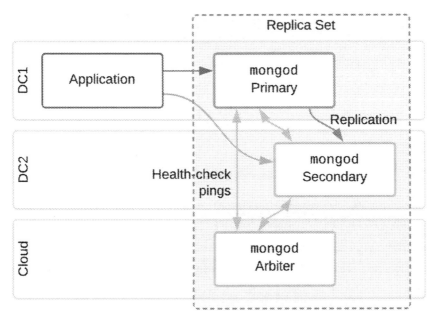

Figure 2-1. *A 2-data center architecture with arbiter*

Hidden secondary

Hidden members are a type of data-bearing node which replicate normally, but are reserved for special workloads such as analytics or data dumps. They can be configured with different indexes and often have different system resources allocated. Hidden nodes can *never become primary* and are *hidden from the client application* (and mongos routers) even for secondary reads.

Applications can connect to these nodes directly for performing aggregation or analytic queries, but should never write to them. Since they replicate from the primary, they may return stale data.

Delayed secondary

Delayed members are a type of hidden member, with a replication delay applied.

Note   Before Ops/Cloud Manager introduced *queryable backups*, these nodes were used to add a level of protection against user error.

Imagine your replica set had an additional node with a 2-hour delay to its replication. In effect, it has a complete copy of the database from 2 hours ago. Now if a database administrator, or application, accidentally deletes or corrupts a complete collection of data, you have a "live backup" available. With some quick human intervention, the application could be pointed to this node, and you've lost only some recent changes. This is a worst-case scenario in production as there are a number of issues as seen in the following steps:

1. You need to discover, decide, and react to the data loss within the 2-hour window.

2. After converting the delayed member to primary, you have lost two hours of other changes.

3. Your application suddenly has a single copy of data if you choose to wipe the other nodes and start an initial sync from this solo node.

4. The new primary is now serving the application and is at the same time the sync source for multiple replications, and so will be significantly loaded.

5. There is likely to be a significant performance impact on the application and end user during recovery.

In Figure 2-2 (left), we see that a forth hidden node replicates with a delay. In case of corruption (right), the delayed node has been converted to a primary, and the other nodes are syncing themselves from this 2-hour old data.

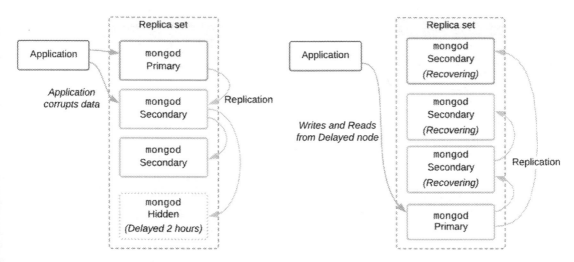

Figure 2-2. *Replica set with a delayed hidden member*

Partial restores

In cases where only some data has been lost, or even an entire collection has been dropped, you could use the delayed member as a clean source. You could dump the collection and restore it back into the replica set. Or you could connect directly to the hidden member and perform a query to retrieve a single document or value.

Note   Hidden nodes should always be added *in addition* to a topology designed for optimal failover. Since they are delayed, they can't participate in majority write acknowledgment and they can't become primary.

Nonvoting secondary

A nonvoting member in a MongoDB replica set has 0 votes but must also have a priority of 0 (meaning it cannot itself become a primary). Replica sets can have at most 7 voting members (to keep the election process as streamlined as possible). Some use cases, however, rely heavily on read operations and don't mind about reading slightly stale data. For such replica sets, the system could scale horizontally by adding more nonvoting secondary nodes.

Note   Secondary reads are not appropriate for most workloads when either (i) data changes frequently or (ii) reading the latest acknowledged data is required.

As shown in Figure 2-3, you can have a large geographically distributed replica set with an even number of nodes in total by using nonvoting secondaries (as long as the number of voting nodes is odd). *Replication chaining* will be used to replicate from fellow secondaries rather than all nodes replicating directly from the primary. This chaining relieves memory and I/O pressure on the primary node, but secondaries will likely suffer significant replication lag. An application reading from secondaries will experience stale reads so this much be supported by the use case.

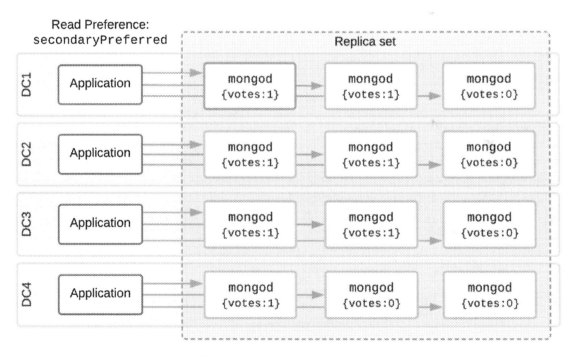

Figure 2-3. *A replica set with many secondaries for scaling reads*

In Table 2-1 we can see an overview of all the node types discussed in this chapter.

Table 2-1. *A summary of different node types*

Type	Settings	Comments
Standard	{votes: 1, priority: 1}	Contains data, can vote, and can become primary.
Arbiter	{votes: 1, priority: 0}	No data so can't become primary, but can vote. Not available on Atlas.
Hidden	{votes: 1, priority: 0, hidden: true}	Contains data, can vote, but can't become primary. Invisible to the client and mongos even for secondary reads.
Delayed	{votes: 1, priority: 0, hidden: true, slaveDelay: 3600}	A special type of hidden node with delayed replication. It can help elect a primary, but since it doesn't have the latest data, *cannot become primary*. Not useful in sharded clusters, and not available on Atlas.
Nonvoting	{votes: 0, priority: 0}	This node replicates data, but doesn't vote nor can it become primary. Useful to ensure an odd number of voting nodes.

Avoiding failure

Any complex system is only as robust as its points of failure. Eventually every component in a system will break down, require an upgrade, a restart, or need to be physically relocated. If the component is the only one of its kind, it is known as a *single point of failure,* or *SPOF*. When it fails, it will break down the entire interdependence of components, leading to application downtime.

To avoid these types of failures, you should have multiple applications running behind a load balancer, on different physical machines and preferably in different data centers. The Domain Name System (DNS) lookup should have multiple nameservers, so that even Internet-level faults should not prevent your users reaching your application server.

When it comes to your MongoDB database, we recommend following the same principle with a replica set with three data-bearing members. This is the minimum to provide both high availability and majority write concerns so that a single node can be lost completely with not only no data loss, but no downtime nor any performance impact whatsoever.

Points of failure

Some common points of failure include

- Data centers (electricity outage, network infrastructure, fire, etc.)

- Physical servers (power supplies, CPUs, storage devices, etc.)

- Software (virtual machine [VM] hosts, operating system crashes)

The risk from some of these points can be greatly reduced with internally redundant systems, such as multiple power supplies, RAID-10 storage with hot-swappable drives, multiple network interface cards, and data centers with backup power and multiple Internet backbones. Automating and testing any failover mechanisms is critical to minimize the downtime and, in an ideal world, avoid it completely.

Reserve capacity

You will want to plan for any component going offline as the worst possible moment. Imagine you have a production workload for a transport provider with 90% of ticket sales occurring at 9–10 a.m. and again at 5–6 p.m. every work day. You should be provisioning your computing resources for MongoDB nodes so that the primary can fail and the replacement primary can handle the same workload.

All this redundancy comes at a price, and system architects and managers must balance the cost of adding redundancy to all these systems. It's tempting to seek clever ways to save money with complex failover strategies with mixed hardware. Later, we will explore a few examples and show why deployments with mixed hardware resources are undesirable.

Automatic failover

Rather than rely solely on redundant hardware, MongoDB offers a simpler and cheaper approach with software that assumes infrastructure failures happen and has failover built-in. By running multiple data-bearing nodes in distinct physical locations, it becomes must less important to ensure that every layer in the infrastructure is resilient. We can run on much less expensive commodity hardware, with a single power supply and single network card, with no backup power or Internet.

If our replica set can handle one or even two complete data center failures simultaneously without data loss, we can save money in infrastructure and provide a database system which can self-heal without any disruption to its application at all.

Most cloud providers include a unified VM interface to customers which appears much the same as running a standard Linux OS on commodity hardware. However, under the covers most cloud providers have built in many layers of redundancy. For example, their network storage solutions are usually built on a RAID-10-style architecture which uses multiple physical storage devices to store each chunk of data and which scales up almost linearly in terms of *IOPS* (input/output operations per second).

Warning   Many cloud providers include storage options with "burst credits." These can be used during workload peaks but will eventually expire. If you see an unexplained sudden drop in IOPS on a cloud VM, it may be that the credit balance reached zero.

Designing for flexibility

Another good way to build fault-tolerant systems is to follow design principles that allow for later flexibility.

DNS not IP

While it is possible to configure your replica set members and seed lists with IP addresses in connection strings (see Figure 2-4), this can make your deployment brittle. By using an internal DNS server, you can give each host in your deployment a logical hostname or alias.

Figure 2-4. *Using IP addresses for configuration results in an inflexible system*

Some organizations will give a host an incremental hostname based on its physical location and business unit, for example, host0003456.mortgages.dc-nyc.bigbank. local. While this is preferable to using an IP address and allows us to quickly see in which data center the host resides, it still lacks flexibility.

If this host formed part of a shard's replica set, and for some reason the motherboard failed completely, this host would need to be replaced. The replacement host would have a new hostname, say host0003587. Now, manual intervention will be required inside the MongoDB deployment for all other members, the mongos, and Ops Manager to know about the new host location for this node's role.

Another approach seen in Figure 2-5 is to give logical naming to the hostname or at least create a CNAME alias to the functional hostname in the form node3.mortgages_ prod.mongo.bigbank.local. In this case, a new host can be spun up, the CNAME alias can be pointed to this hostname, the mongod processes configured, and all components will be able to discover it automatically as soon as the DNS cache flushes. For planned migrations, the DNS time-to-live (TTL) can be shortened to reduce the cache duration.

Figure 2-5. *Using logical hostnames makes it easier to understand and manage complex deployment; it also makes it easier to replace failed hosts*

Note   For the auto-discovery features of replica set, sharded cluster, and Ops Manager agents, each node needs to detect its own "MongoDB hostname" as the host's fully qualified hostname (FQDN). The result of the command hostname -f should always match the name of the node in configuration. On Linux, this can be achieved by running hostnamectl set-hostname <new_hostname> or changing the hostname in /etc/hostname and restarting the host. Failing to check this can mean that a mongod doesn't know its own identity.

Auto-discovery

MongoDB drivers will automatically try to detect all members of a deployment. Even if you list only one member of a replica set in the connection URI string, a driver will still establish connections to all members to react faster to elections and other replica set changes. However, you should always include all known replica set members or mongos routers in the connection URI in case the listed nodes are unavailable when the application first starts.

Planned downtime

The inherently distributed nature of MongoDB replica sets means that it is perfectly normal and expected that nodes will be taken down intentionally from time to time for planned maintenance. As long as any maintenance doesn't take longer than the oplog window, a node will automatically catch up any changes upon restart.

There is no need to reconfigure a replica set for planned downtime. It is better to leave configuration in place, so that the node is automatically and instantly rejoined to the set once it is restarted.

Note   It is strongly recommended to leverage rolling upgrades to keep your MongoDB nodes running on the *latest minor release* of the current major version. As with any software, occasionally bugs are found that affect stability or security. Avoid your deployment being taken offline by a bug that has already been fixed, and update quickly.

Multiple routers

Any sharded cluster used in production should have at least two mongos router nodes in the deployment (see Figure 2-6). The application should be configured with all mongos instances in the connection URI string to support failover. The mongos will connect to each shard much the same as an application connects to a replica set. And in the same way that the drivers discover all replica set members, the mongos will auto-discover all components in the sharded cluster via the config servers.

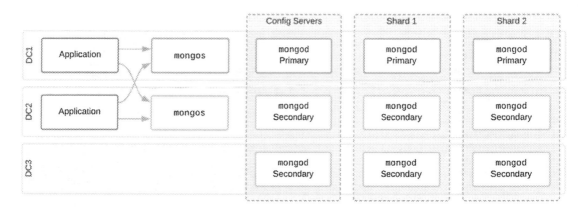

Figure 2-6. *Highly available deployment with multiple mongos nodes*

For deployments with multiple application servers, a good option is to keep a mongos collocated with the app server. This reduces latency for cases when a mongos is piping data to the application. Since the mongos is generally not stateful and doesn't persist any data on disk, they can be spun up and down as required by load. If you have an application running inside a cloud "auto-scaling group" which spins up a new virtual machine during peak load, you should include a mongos in that prebuilt image, so your shard routers will scale automatically too.

Each mongos will maintain a connection with every other mongos, as well as each nonhidden node in the deployment. In Figure 2-7, each mongos will keep 9 connections open, each taking about 1MB of RAM per node. Imagine a large deployment with 30 mongoses and 10 shards, each with 5 nodes. In such a deployment, each mongos opens almost 80 connections just to maintain a constant health check of all components in the deployment. For this reason, we normally recommend to not exceed 30 mongoses in a deployment and instead vertically scale up a fixed-size pool of mongoses with additional memory and CPU resources.

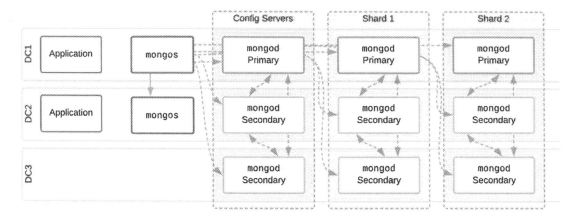

Figure 2-7. *Sharded cluster showing the open connections for one mongos*

Rolling maintenance

One important way to avoid failure during planned maintenance or configuration changes is to apply them one node at a time. Since a well-designed replica set can function with one member offline, we should perform operations such as version upgrades in a *rolling manner*.

Some operations such as index builds are best performed on nodes temporarily separated from the set. This can be achieved by stopping a node, temporarily starting it without its replica set parameters. This node will still have a copy of the data, but will be invisible to the application and the other replica set members. Once the index build is complete, the node can be restarted with its replication parameters and rejoin the set. Many other operations such as a binary version upgrades or certain server configuration options (security, performance, etc.) require a node restart.

While these rolling maintenance operations can be performed manually or via scripts, the automation features of Ops/Cloud Manager have been specifically designed to perform these operations. Changes are made node by node, with all secondaries being changed first, and only if successful at that point, the primary node will be *stepped down* before making changes so that the write workload is not affected. Automation will never start rolling maintenance if the cluster is unhealthy, such as if one node is already unavailable. It will also never take down another node for maintenance if the previous node's changes are not complete and successful. This avoids reducing the resilience or availability of a replica set unnecessarily.

Clean step-down

The *step-down* is an explicit signal by a primary to other members of the replica set (and any clients connected) that an election will be taking place. It triggers an election immediately and much more smoothly than a sudden loss of a primary under heavy load. With this notification, an election can occur in milliseconds. If the elected node hasn't yet caught up to the old secondary, it will first catch up before it can accept any new writes (see the `catchUpTimeoutMillis` setting). If it hasn't caught up within 30 seconds, the old primary which is still the most up to date will call a new election to take over, to ensure that the set isn't blocking incoming writes.

Since the application will hold and retry any pending operations until a new primary is ready, this means the application impact is also extremely short and completely transparent to end users.

Without a step-down, secondaries will, by default, wait 10 seconds (the `electionTimeoutMillis` setting in the replica set configuration) before triggering an election. This is to avoid unnecessary changes of primary due to very brief network errors or stalls.

Tooling failover

Ops/Cloud Manager is an automation, monitoring, and backup tool available to MongoDB Enterprise customers that provides crucial features for managing complex sharded clusters in private data centers. As such, it is critical for this tool to have similar redundancy and automatic failover.

Figure 2-8 shows an example of an Ops Manager deployment with good redundancies in place. Any of the data centers can be lost without any application downtime. The Ops Manager application itself has a hot backup, so that Automation and monitoring can continue automatically. The backup snapshots are kept in an S3-compatible storage solution on-prem which is itself configured over multiple data centers. Only the Backup Daemon is lacking automatic failover. If DC1 is lost, manual intervention is required to activate a Backup Daemon as part of the Ops Manager instance in DC2.

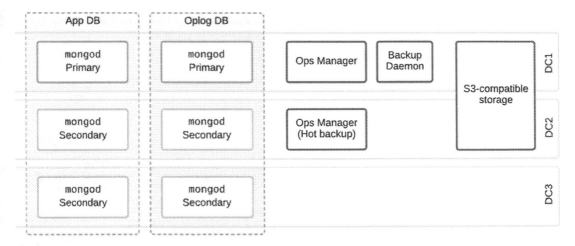

Figure 2-8. *A deployment using Ops Manager (Enterprise only) with redundancy*

Failure scenarios

As in any complex, distributed system, there are many possible problems that may arise to affect the availability of a production database. With redundant nodes, losing a single server or the corruption of an entire filesystem does not mean that data is lost or that a database is unavailable.

However, there are a number of common errors which without correct fault-tolerant design may lead to unexpected or undesirable states.

Network partition

When you have a database distributed over multiple data centers connected by a network backbone, there is a risk that the connection between the data DCs will fail intermittently or even for an extended period. We want to avoid data corruption or inconsistency at all costs, so in certain situations the deployment will automatically switch to read-only mode to avoid a situation with the same document is edited simultaneously in two different places.

Let's consider an example illustrated in Figure 2-9. Here, we have access only to two data centers – one is considered a "Production" site and the other a "disaster recovery" site. Based on this design philosophy, the secondary in DC2 is primarily intended as a reserve for disaster recovery purposes. It might be that the priority of the nodes has been adjusted so that the nodes in DC1 have a higher priority, effectively preventing node

3 from ever becoming the primary. As we can see in the diagram, a network partition simply disconnects a single member. A *quorum* (a majority of voting nodes) is present in DC1 so an election is not necessary, and the primary does not need to change.

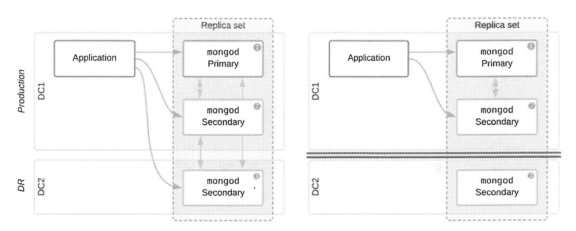

Figure 2-9. *(Left) A replica set with a single member in DC2. (Right) A network partition disconnects the DC2 node*

Now let's consider an example with two application servers in Figure 2-10. These might be configured with a load balancer, or perhaps users near DC2 use that application server based on some custom routing. Should a network failure partition DC1 from DC2, an election will occur inside DC1 and a new primary elected there. The application in DC2 will still be able to read old data from its local node, but will neither be able to write nor receive any update from the primary.

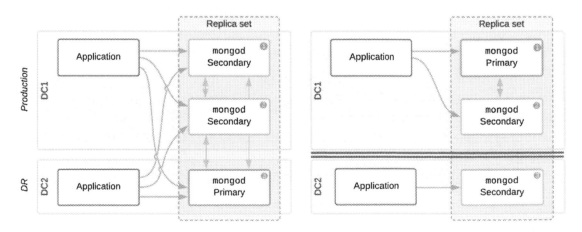

Figure 2-10. *(Left) A deployment with a secondary application server. (Right) A network partition means the secondary application server can read only*

Hardware failure

To all other members of a replica set, a member node going offline due to a hardware or software failure is the same as if that node has lost network access. Figure 2-11 shows that an election will take place, and the two nodes still in communication with each other have a quorum to hold an election. The application servers will automatically reconnect to the new primary to retry any pending writes.

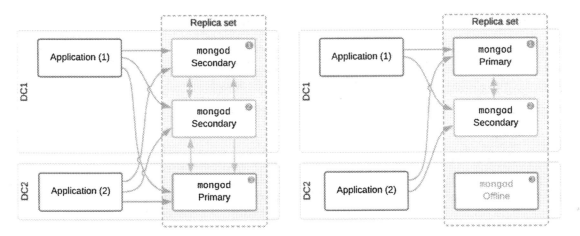

Figure 2-11. *(Left) A primary in alone in DC2. (Right) A failed host/node will cause an election but no downtime*

Remote DC failure

Another common scenario particularly for internal applications is that the databases run within corporate data centers but that applications run somewhere else – an office network or from employees' personal computers. Figure 2-12 is an example where a "production" data center DC1 with a majority of nodes goes offline. From the perspective of the Application and node 3, the effective outcome of the network partition is identical to if nodes 1 and 2 crashed simultaneously. However, from inside DC1, the primary remains unchanged since those two nodes can still form a quorum. The problem arises if the application had been writing changes (even with majority write concern) at the same moment. Nodes 1 and 2 could have acknowledged some writes that may not yet have replicated to node 3. If the application reads from the secondary in DC2, it will miss those writes.

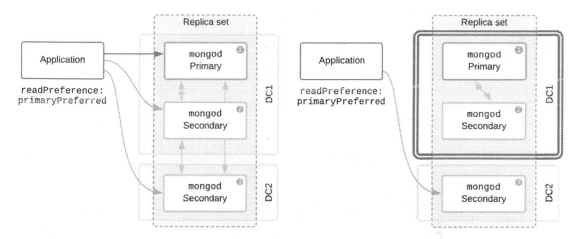

Figure 2-12. *A remote application will connect to a secondary and perform reads if* `primaryPreferred` *read preference is configured*

With manual intervention, we could reconfigure the replica set on node 3 and remove nodes 1 and 2 completely from the member list. That would allow node 3 to become primary as the only node left, but some writes will have been lost and make it impossible to integrate the changes when DC1 comes back online.

This is another example of why a 3-DC configuration is preferable. Even an entire DC down would never mean a lack of quorum and no need for manual intervention.

Storage volume failure

One less common and harder to handle problem is if there is an issue with the storage volume which prevents timely I/O but which is not serious enough to prevent the node from functioning at all. Imagine a subtle hardware failure in the storage device in Figure 2-13. Instead of operating at its usual capacity of 2000 I/O operations per second (IOPS), it suddenly is only performing 200 IOPS (or is stalling and then working in short bursts). As a member of a replica set, it still responds to pings and passes all health checks. As such there is no reason to trigger an election. Instead the replica set can now only service incoming writes at 10% of its previous capacity level.

47

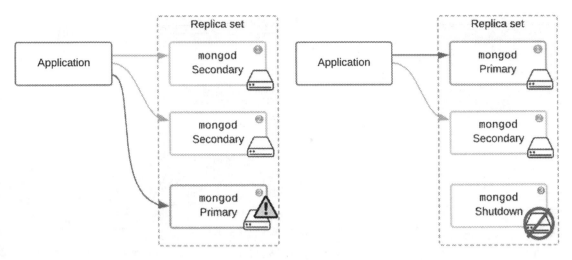

Figure 2-13. *The Storage Node Watchdog will take a node offline if its storage becomes unresponsive*

One partial solution is the *Storage Node Watchdog* (which became available in the Community version of MongoDB since 4.2). This is an optional service which monitors the health of the filesystems on its node and, upon detecting an unresponsive filesystem, will trigger a shutdown of the node. In the case that this node is the primary, it will also cause an election to take place, effectively passing the responsibility of handling writes to another member of the replica set.

Network degradation

A similar scenario to earlier can occur due to a failing network where some packet drops affect bandwidth (Figure 2-14). Since the health check pings eventually succeed thanks to TCP retries, an election is not triggered. With MongoDB, elections incur a cost in terms of connection churn and application retries and so the algorithm avoids stepping down a primary unless it is sure that there is a better candidate. In this case, it's up to the network administrators to set up monitoring and alerts on the network infrastructure itself. In such an event, a database administrator may choose to trigger a step-down or adjust member priorities while the network is being stabilized.

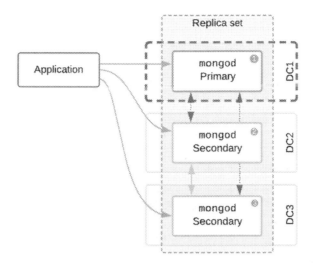

Figure 2-14. *Node in DC1 experiences degraded network but remains primary*

Shared VM hosts

It is now very common for enterprises to use VM hosts when deploying applications in their on-prem data centers. This adds an extra level of complexity since noisy neighbors can steal resources or misconfigurations can lead to suboptimal memory use (such as memory overcommitment or excess memory swapping). In addition to those performance issues, co-locating multiple MongoDB nodes from the same replica set can co-join points of failure. For example, in Figure 2-15 we see that a majority of nodes reside on single physical VM host. Should this host suffer a hardware fault or be shut down for urgent maintenance, these two nodes will suddenly fail together and the set will become read-only.

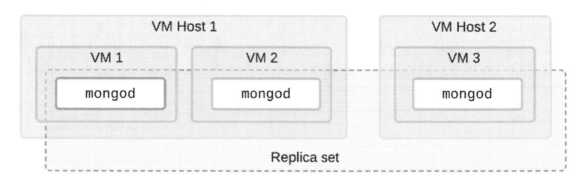

Figure 2-15. *Nodes co-located on the same VM host add a joint point of failure*

Shared storage area network

Another possibly unexpected point of failure is the "inverted pyramid" of shared network storage. In many cases of virtual host configurations, there is a shared storage server connected by fiber channel, but which is shared by multiple VM hosts (Figure 2-16). Even though each MongoDB node has independent physical CPUs and memory, should the SAN fail, all nodes will fail also. Once again, having three separate data centers completely avoids this failure scenario.

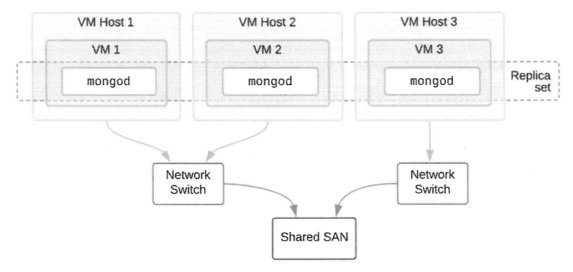

Figure 2-16. *A shared SAN can introduce an unexpected point of failure*

Unbalanced hardware

Imagine a situation where the primary is designed to be co-located in the first data center with the application server to reduce latency. This node is given a priority so it should win elections when all nodes are available. It's given more memory and CPUs since it will be handling writes and reads from the application. The other nodes are given less resources. The node in the secondary data center is even given priority 0 to ensure that it never gets elected primary (see Figure 2-17).

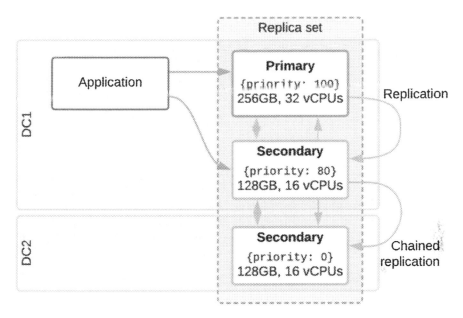

Figure 2-17. *A replica set with a designated primary with double the memory and CPU resources*

Now let's imagine what happens if the primary host fails. The secondary in DC1 is elected primary, but it has half the resources of the old primary. It can only fit half the previous cache in memory; it will have to do much more I/O to flush dirty caches and load data from disk. The effect will be that write performance drops to significantly below half the previous level. It is very likely that the application performance will suffer noticeably to the end users.

In Figure 2-18 we have given the secondary in DC1 the same resources, and now only the node in DC2 has half the resources. Now if the primary fails, the secondary in DC1 will again be elected to replace it, and can function the same, but if the application is using *majority write concern* to avoid rollbacks, it is now waiting for the only other available node to replicate the writes. Since the oplog entries must be applied in order, any processing lag in the underresourced secondary will now make the application wait. In effect, the application is still waiting on a node with half the resources to write all the same changes and update all the same indexes.

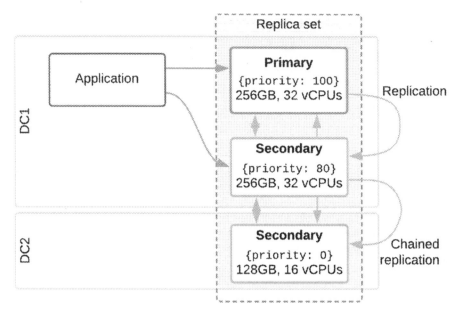

Figure 2-18. *A replica set with an underprovisioned secondary kept as reserve*

We have seen that replication and majority write concern are two major reasons to avoid having unbalanced node resources in production. For three-node replica sets, your deployment's capacity is limited by the computing resources of the slowest node after any single component failure.

Key takeaways

From this chapter, the key concepts to remember are as follows:

- The MongoDB architecture has been designed to optimize both uptime and recovery.

- Mitigation steps can be taken to avoid failure by adding redundant components and avoid single points of failure in the infrastructure.

- Deploying a replica set with an odd number of nodes in at least three data centers with multiple internet backbones should avoid many points of failure.

- Special nodes such as hidden or delayed members should only be deployed in additional to at least three data-bearing nodes.

- It is impossible to have multiple primaries in a replica set. Because a quorum of voting nodes is required for a primary, only one side of the partition can win an election. With an even number of voting nodes, it is possible for neither side to have a primary despite all nodes being online.

- Manual intervention should be avoided and planned away. By following the best practices, the only time that manual intervention should be required is if multiple independent failures occur concurrently.

- Rolling maintenance should be used to upgrade or change configuration so that only one node is unavailable at any time.

- All nodes in a replica set should be configured with an oplog of at least 72 hours to allow for fast recovery and SLAs to be met even over a weekend.

CHAPTER 3

Security

In 2016, Cybersecurity Ventures, a US research firm, predicted that cyber-crime will cost the world $6 trillion annually by 2021, up from $3 trillion in 2015.[1]

This chapter looks at the main security features related to MongoDB cluster designs, including how to secure a system at the infrastructure level, and to encrypt data in transit and at rest, and how to protect against attacks via application code and interfaces.

Finally, we look at how to audit cluster actions and to obfuscate logs to allow performance analysis without leaking user data out of the database.

Local access

The first step to securing any MongoDB deployment is to ensure that access to the host machine is restricted to only trusted users. Since all data is ultimately stored on the filesystem, a malicious system user could corrupt, steal, hold hostage, or destroy any data stored on the local disk.

Each operating system has its own methods to restrict logins to a machine. Normally each user would have their own authentication credentials (a password or SSH key) and be assigned to a group. The `mongod` process and its binary and data files typically run as `mongod:mongod` which is the default when MongoDB is installed on a Linux machine via an RPM archive.

As a sysadmin, you should always follow the *principle of least privilege,* for example, by disallowing root SSH access into a machine, limiting `sudo` privileges, and logging to record all connections attempts both successful and failed for later auditing. Security resources like OWASP (`www.owasp.org`) provide useful tools and training to help.

---

[1]`www.pwc.com/m1/en/publications/documents/wgs-cybersecurity-paper-new-updates.pdf`

© Nicholas Cottrell 2020

N. Cottrell, *MongoDB Topology Design*, https://doi.org/10.1007/978-1-4842-5817-0_3

Network hardening

Once MongoDB is running on a host, it will need to communicate with other members of its replica set or sharded cluster (in both directions) and will need to receive certain incoming connections from other trusted sources such as applications and data exploration tools like MongoDB Compass. There are many layers of security which we will cover later, but at the most basic, we want to restrict access to only certain ports and limit to certain remote hosts.

As shown in Figure 3-1, all replica set components and the driver will need to be able to establish outgoing connections and communicate with all other components, usually across data centers.

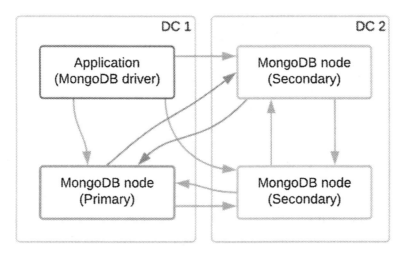

Figure 3-1. *Connections established by components in a replica set*

Firewalls with iptables

Most Linux flavors include a firewall system preinstalled. We will cover the most common one: iptables. This is a very complex and powerful firewall system which can be difficult to configure correctly. Red Hat Linux includes some helper tools both in the graphical user interface and a wizard to help generate a list of rules for iptables.

In fact, you can configure your firewall manually using a set of blocks to build up rules to allow connections to and from only other members of the MongoDB cluster and any application servers, developer machines, or even end-user hosts.

To allow incoming connections from trusted hosts, you can add entries to the configuration files /etc/sysconfig/iptables (and /etc/sysconfig/ip6tables) like Listing 3-1.

Listing 3-1. Allow traffic through the firewall for trusted host 12.34.56.78

```
-A INPUT -s 12.34.56.78 -j ACCEPT
-A OUTPUT -d 12.34.56.78 -j ACCEPT
```

This will allow any traffic (TCP or UDP) on any port from and to this trusted host. For additional security, you could also limit to only TCP traffic on the port the MongoDB node is using. In addition, you can limit outgoing traffic to only connections that were established from the remote host as shown in Listing 3-2.

Listing 3-2. Allow only TCP traffic for the active MongoDB port

```
-A INPUT -s 12.34.56.78 -p tcp --destination-port 27017 -m state --state
NEW,ESTABLISHED -j ACCEPT
-A OUTPUT -d 12.34.56.78 -p tcp --source-port 27017 -m state --state
ESTABLISHED -j ACCEPT
```

You will need this configuration pair for every host in your deployment, including config servers, mongos instances, and any host running an application which needs to connect to the database.

In order to make sure that iptables is running, restart it with the following:

```
service iptables restart
```

If your network or hosts support IPv6, you can either configure ip6tables also or disable IPv6 completely for this host and configure MongoDB to bind only to IPv4 network interfaces.

You could also use firewalld as an alternative to iptables for newer Linux systems. Both utilize the netfilter framework for the actual processing of packets, but firewalld can change configurations on already open connections. For troubleshooting connection issues on Linux, ss -plnt can be useful for seeing socket statistics.

On Windows, you can use netsh to open up all required ports between all components (all MongoDB nodes, shard and config servers, and application). As always, the documentation provides step-by-step examples for your version of MongoDB.

Limit interfaces with bindIp

By default, recent versions of MongoDB default the `bindIp` configuration parameter to `127.0.0.1`. This means the `mongod` process only listens to incoming requests from the `localhost` interface and ignores any external network interfaces. This is fine for testing on a development machine, or running a standalone MongoDB on the same cloud server instance as a web server. To accept a request from an external client, you would need to also specify the IP address of the interface, that is, the IP address assigned to the host by the network which is used for routing external traffic by setting:

```
net:
  bindIp: 12.34.56.78
```

If for some reason your host is allocated dynamic IP addresses which change over time, you could allow MongoDB to bind to all interfaces by adding:

```
net:
  bindIp: 0.0.0.0
```

or

```
net:
  bindIpAll: true
```

Note   This could allow incoming connection attempts from the Internet. You should always enable authentication before adding external interfaces.

Customize ports

Another small security enhancement is to run your MongoDB deployment on nonstandard ports. In a sharded cluster, by default, data-bearing nodes will run on port 27018 and `mongoses` on 27017. By moving these to different ports, naïve malware or port scanners may be prevented from detecting running MongoDB instances.

These can be configured in the config file with

```
net:
  port: 37001
```

Filesystem

On most Linux installs, MongoDB runs as user mongod and group mongod. Therefore, it creates all data files and logs as this same mongod user. Both the data files and log files path should also be owned by the user and group, and all other users should not even have read access.

Current permissions can be checked by running ls -l on your dbPath, which is typically /var/lib/mongodb.

If you create a keyfile to secure the server, it should also be owned by mongod and not even have read access by group. This can be achieved by running:

```
chmod 600 /path/to/keyfile
```

Note   Without file-level encryption, anyone with root access to the host could launch a separate mongod process with no access control and read the data.

Authentication

While network-level security is a key factor in securing any database, it forms only one part of any secure environment. Connections from known sources still need to be limited to prevent compromised hosts accessing data remotely. MongoDB supports a myriad of different authentication methods to require new incoming connections to identify themselves before performing any database operations.

Passwords vs. keyfiles

Creating users with rule-based access control (RBAC) in MongoDB deployments is highly recommended, and you should create at least one user account as soon as you start storing any real data in your database.

Like most databases, you can create a username and password which can be granted access to multiple databases or collections. Users can be restricted to certain roles such as "read only" or limited to be able to configure the replica set, but cannot see any data at all. You should always follow the principle of "least privilege" and only grant roles that this particular user needs to complete their use cases.

> **Note**   Creating a user account is not enough to require authentication when connecting to a MongoDB database. You must also explicitly enable authentication.

Authentication can be enabled by adding the following lines to the config file and then restarting the MongoDB node:

```
security:
    authorization: enabled
```

Access controls can be temporarily disabled by a system administrator by restarting the mongod process without the --auth parameter or security.authorization config. This can be useful for maintenance and password resets if the admin password is lost.

Connecting with passwords

When connecting to MongoDB from a driver or a data explorer tool like MongoDB Compass or the Mongo shell, you need to supply both the username and password either via a special field or in the *connection URI* in the form:

```
mongodb://[username:password@]host1[:port1][,...hostN[:portN]][/[database]
[?options]]
```

When specifying passwords with special characters in the URI, they will need to be escaped, and when used on the command line, they should be surrounded by double or single quotes.

One of the problems of using passwords in a deployment is that scripts will need to store passwords to connect to MongoDB. This is a security risk since passwords exist unencrypted inside script files (and source control) and may appear in the process list (e.g., ps on Linux) and may be stored insecurely on user's personal computers.

If your organization has stricter security requirements, you should consider x.509 certificates (discussed later).

Keyfiles

The keyfile is in essence a very long password stored in a secure file and referenced by each mongod node in the deployment. This keyfile acts as a "shared secret" between the components and lets them authenticate themselves when establishing a replica set, or when adding a brand-new node to an existing set.

Without this shared secret, it could be possible for hackers to add a new empty node under their control into an existing replica set and trigger an initial sync. They would then be piggybacking onto the MongoDB replication architecture to make a copy of the database.

The contents of these files should be treated as a password and read access restricted at the filesystem level. Anyone with the contents could spoof access to the replica set and so this is a bare-minimum security approach for your deployment.

You can instruct MongoDB to require a keyfile for internal authentication by indicating the path as follows and restarting the server:

```
security:
    keyFile: /path/secure.key
```

Note that setting a keyfile will automatically enable authentication too.

x.509 certificates

A superior but more complex method than using a keyfile is to create and deploy x.509 certifications for your server and client components.

At the time of writing, there's a convenient free site called Let's Encrypt that makes it easy to generate x.509 certificates that can be used with MongoDB, but requires that your hosts have publicly addressable DNS hostnames. These certificates only last 90 days, so you will want to script their generation and renewal.

While x.509 certificates can be used to secure *internal* communication between MongoDB cluster components, a slightly different certificate format can be used for *application* clients to authenticate themselves with the clusters. If you chose to use this method, then each different user account connecting needs to have a unique certificate created for it with the username embedded in the metadata.

Client authentication

MongoDB has separate subsystems for *authentication* and *authorization*. Authentication can be performed using a built-in authentication method called Salted Challenge Response Authentication Mechanism (SCRAM) or via an external authentication system that supports Lightweight Directory Access Protocol (LDAP) or Kerberos. With SCRAM, users and their credentials are stored encrypted in the admin database (and replicated automatically to all members in a deployment).

Authorization is a subsequent step after authentication is successful, in which MongoDB will check the authenticated user's roles and privileges before allowing a command to be run.

Authorization can be granted at a database or collection level as required. Multiple predefined roles' permissions can be added together to achieve the right mix.

Note   x.509 and Kerberos integrations allow only for authentication, and the authorization is based on privileges and roles created on the `admin` database. MongoDB Enterprise also supports full authorization via LDAP – so that both users and roles are fully defined inside an LDAP server.

External authentication

There are several types of external authentication methods available with MongoDB. As of this writing, supported methods include x.509, LDAP, and Kerberos. LDAP is a standard directory protocol with many open source and commercial implementations such as OpenLDAP, Windows Active Directory, and Apache Directory Server. Kerberos is an industry-standard authentication protocol for large client/server systems, allowing both the client and server to verify each other's identities. At the time of writing, Kerberos is supported in Windows Active Directory and Apache Directory Server.

Most of these methods require creating a user on the `$external` database and defining roles and privileges inside MongoDB. The external source performs only the authentication step.

When using external authentication, it is the MongoDB server which communicates with the external authentication service, not the application directly (Figure 3-2).

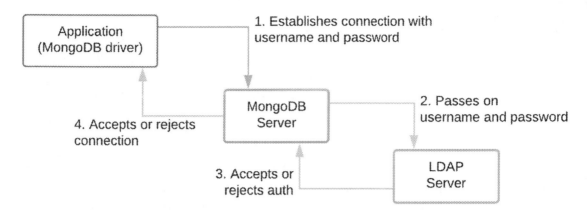

Figure 3-2. *Steps and communication for external authentication*

Table 3-1 lists the supported auth mechanisms and how they relate to authentication and authorization behavior. The value for configuring the mechanism via --authenticationMechanism is shown in brackets. Note that even when using Kerberos authentication, you can still use LDAP authorization for mapping users to roles.

Table 3-1. *Different auth mechanisms available*

Mechanism	Authentication	Authorization
SCRAM (SCRAM-SHA-256)	Password encrypted inside MongoDB	Privileges defined in MongoDB.
x.509 (MONGODB-X.509, external)	User registered but no password in MongoDB. Each user has a unique certificate.	
LDAP (PLAIN, external)	Client sends password, but password is never stored in MongoDB.	Privileges defined in MongoDB or works with an LDAP for optional authorization (MongoDB Enterprise only).
Kerberos (GSSAPI, external)	User registered but no password in MongoDB.	

Encrypted connections

Even if all your MongoDB nodes and applications exist inside the same secure network, it's still a good idea to consider encrypting all communications. This can prevent eavesdropping on network traffic to/from your MongoDB deployment and make it easier to scale out should you want to migrate later. For example, you may want to gradually transition from a fully on-prem setup to a hybrid solution with some nodes hosted on a cloud provider.

For any production use, you should already be considering a multi-data center configuration for your MongoDB deployment with physically separated data centers. Even with VPNs/VPCs, you will almost always be relying on shared Internet backbones between data centers for keeping these components in sync, and so again encrypted connections are critical to keep your data safe.

MongoDB Community edition includes full encryption for data *in transit* using TLS/ SSL (transport encryption). Since encrypted connections are critical for a secure system, recent versions of MongoDB have removed support for older, less secure TLS 1.0 systems by default. You can use any valid certificate from an official *certificate authority*, or you can build your own *self-signed certificates* from scratch using the openssl command-line tool. With either approach, the data stream will be encrypted, but without the identity validation of having your certificates signed by a third-party certificate authority, your communication may be vulnerable to a so-called *man-in-the-middle attack*.

Even when you have configured TLS for your internal MongoDB communications, you need to explicitly enable encryption from your application to MongoDB by adding ?ssl=true to the connection string. If you want to require all clients to use TLS to be able to connect to your MongoDB server, you can add this to your MongoDB configuration:

```
net:
  tls:
    mode:      requireTLS
```

Note   In MongoDB 4.2 and later, all configuration references were changed from SSL to TLS, for example,

```
net.ssl.mode: requireSSL
```

became

```
net.tls.mode: requireTLS
```

In production environments, you should be using valid certificates for all components in the MongoDB deployment which have been signed by the *same certificate authority* (either an internal organization-wide one or a trusted third-party TLS vendor).

TLS 1.2

Some organizations have strict requirements that TLS 1.2 be used to encrypt all connections. If this is the case, you can explicitly disable TLS 1.0 and 1.1 in MongoDB, by adding the `disabledProtocols` parameter to any MongoDB server with SSL/TLS already enabled:

```
net:
  tls:
    disabledProtocols: TLS1_0,TLS1_1
```

In many of the drivers, you can also force TLS 1.2 for outgoing application connections. For example, with the Java driver you can enforce TLS 1.2 by building a connection with the following code:

```
SSLContext sslContext = SSLContext.getInstance("TLSv1.2");
MongoClientOptions options = MongoClientOptions.builder()
                  .sslEnabled(true)
                  .sslInvalidHostNameAllowed(true)
                  .socketFactory(sslContext.getSocketFactory())
                  .build();
```

Encryption at rest

By default, MongoDB stores its data on disk in the form of WiredTiger binary files compressed by snappy. If an unauthorized party were to gain access to these files (or a backup of them) with no encryption, they could easily launch their own local MongoDB process pointing to those files and launch a database, with all authentication disabled. Then any MongoDB client could connect to browse or query that data.

To protect against this sort of attack, any MongoDB database containing real user data should be encrypting data at rest.

Data-at-rest encryption can be solved with either of the following approaches:

1. Encrypt the volume

2. Encrypt from the application

The first item can be solved with disk encryption on the filesystem. If you are self-hosting on a major cloud provider, you should have access to a filesystem-level encryption which leverages the built-in master key management services.

Alternatively, all recent enterprise Linux versions include full-disk encryption solutions such as Linux Unified Key Setup-on-disk-format (or LUKS). This also employs a master key for encrypting entire storage volumes or a subset. You should store your MongoDB data files on a separate volume to the root partition (to allow targeted performance tuning), and this also makes filesystem-level encryption a practical option.

However, if you don't want to encrypt at the volume level, then encryption inside the database server itself is the other option.

Luckily encryption at rest is an optional module for the Enterprise version of MongoDB. This encryption process happens completely automatically. Only encrypted data is ever written to disk, while unencrypted data is available only inside the host's memory.

Note   Any core/memory dumps when an application crashes may contain unencrypted MongoDB data, so be careful when sharing dumps with third parties.

By configuring encryption with an external master key and proper key rotation using a third-party Key Management Interoperability Protocol (KMIP)-compatible key management application, most data privacy compliance regulations will be satisfied.

Backups

You should not forget to ensure that any backups taken are also encrypted and stored securely. When using mongodump for backups, you could write to an encrypted volume. If you are using Ops Manager for backups, then a KMIP-compatible key server is required for snapshots to be encrypted.

Auditing, obfuscation of logs

Since MongoDB 2.6, the Enterprise version of MongoDB has included an auditing feature. When enabled on the mongod or mongos instances, this allows database administrators to track all key changes to complex deployments. These audit logs can be critical when performing a postmortem after any sort of security event, or as part of regular compliance checks. In these situations, the audit log could show any changes to users' roles, new users created, or unexpected access to production databases.

There is no equivalent Community version of this auditing functionality, although third parties have created solutions that replicate some basic features, including filtering output to particular users, database, collection, or source location.

The audit log functionality needs to be explicitly enabled in the MongoDB configuration file and can be piped to a file, the console, or to a compatible syslog destination for eventually storage on a centralized log server for added security. Once activated it will, by default, record a log entry for every change action by any user in the deployment. Filters can also be configured to streamline the audit log.

An example of a simple configuration is shown in Listing 3-3.

Listing 3-3. Enables audit logging in BSON format

```
auditLog:
    destination: file
    format: BSON
    path: /var/lib/mongodb/auditLog.bson
```

Storing the audit log on the same filesystem as the node and its data has considerable drawbacks. For example, the log file needs to have read/write permissions by the mongod process. Should the server be compromised by an external hacker or even a staff member with credentials, they could cover their tracks by removing evidence from the auditLog.bson file or deleting the file completely to make post-mortems impossible.

Another approach would be to pipe auditing logs through syslog and install a *log processing system* such as **rsyslog** which can handle different log generating sources and output them into different outputs. This would involve setting up a *Rsyslog client* on the MongoDB host machine and a centralized *Rsyslog server* which accepts log messages from every host in your deployment via an open TCP port. From the MongoDB side, this requires changing the configuration settings to

```
auditLog:
   destination: syslog
```

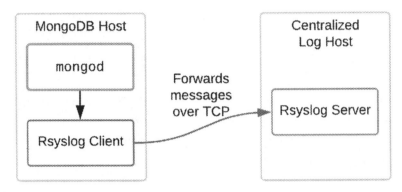

Figure 3-3. *Auditing log messages sent to a centralized host*

Note   A separate MongoDB deployment is actually a possible output destination for `rsyslog` and can be a great option for centralizing logging from complex application deployments, but it's probably better to keep MongoDB audit logs in a completely separate architecture to avoid tampering of audit trails.

By default, log files are neither encrypted nor obfuscated, but there is another Enterprise feature for redacting possible user data bleeding into the log files. To enable this set

```
security:
   redactClientLogData: true
```

in the config file, or enable at runtime with

```
db.adminCommand(
   { setParameter: 1, redactClientLogData : true | false }
)
```

Proactive security

For any secure network, you should already have in place regular physical and environmental security reviews, vulnerability scanning, penetration testing, and automatic alerting of abnormal traffic patterns on network of virtual machines. This should allow for quick intervention for any security breaches.

MongoDB supports most versions for about 2 years after release, with regular security patches. You should quickly upgrade to any minor releases (such as from 4.2.8 to 4.2.9) since these often include security improvements but never introduce breaking compatibility changes. You could also consider moving to the latest major version upgrade within 6 months of release to benefit from other major security and stability improvements.

You could also monitor `www.mongodb.com/alerts` where critical alerts and advisories will be posted.

Server-side JavaScript

Input validation and injection attacks

Since MongoDB is based around JSON documents, there is no risk from traditional *SQL injection attacks*. However, there is a possibility of *JSON injection attacks* especially when running JavaScript/NodeJS web applications (like the Mongoose ORM) or APIs. Imagine an API which accepts a JSON document as part of a query. If this query were to be passed directly to a MongoDB `find` query, a malicious user might be able to use tricks of MongoDB query language to query data belonging to other users, known as "object injection." Known attacks use a combination of `$not` and `$ne` to bypass normal checks.

Imagine that you had a login screen that accepted a web browser input in the form:

```
{user: 'nic', password; '123'}
```

And this was passed directly into a query such as

```
db.users.findOne(query)
```

69

If this `findOne` returned a result, we have authenticated the user and loaded their data in one step. Clever approach to reduce a round-trip to the server? No. If a hacker were to send instead

```
{user: 'nic', password: {$ne: ''}}
```

or

```
{user: 'nic', password: {$gt: ''}}
```

this would also return a document to the `findOne` query without the hacker having to even attempt to guess my password. Of course, this sort of attack does not just apply to reading unauthorized data. Even inserts and updates into a database from applications that don't validate JSON data could be possible.

Therefore, for application designers accepting JSON documents in API queries, it is critical to validate such documents and extract values in their expected data type.

For NodeJS, there are some libraries such as Joi[2] which can help. Other options include using `JSON.parse`, using an `npm` package like `mongo-sanitize`, or manually removing any dollar signs or curly brackets in API input before using the data.

$where operator

The `$where` operator is an old `find` query feature which lets you pass either a string containing a JavaScript expression or a full JavaScript function to the query subsystem. Obviously allowing JavaScript commands to be passed to the internal JavaScript engine included in MongoDB is dangerous, especially if there's a risk that this could come from unvalidated user input.

There have been various security improvements and limitations added to restrict its impact, but the bottom line is that this is a very dangerous feature and almost every original use case can be handled by other more recent, performant, secure MongoDB functions.

Even in the latest versions of MongoDB, this option is enabled by default, but we recommend that you disable it in all deployments by adding

```
security:
    javascriptEnabled: false
```

---

[2]https://github.com/hapijs/joi

to your configuration file or using the `--noscripting` command-line option. This will also disable the old `mapReduce` and `db.collection.group` function – both of which can be replaced in your application with the use of the aggregation pipeline.

Note   If you have SELinux enabled, you should definitely disable server-side JavaScript since attempts to run any operations requiring JavaScript will result in MongoDB segmentation fault.

SELinux

Security-Enhanced Linux (also known as *SELinux*) is a Linux module that provides a mechanism for supporting access control security policies, such as mandatory access controls. Once enabled, SELinux can prevent any individual program/service on a Linux host from compromising the entire system by limiting access to certain preapproved directories, files, and network ports.

When setting up MongoDB, you can run SELinux in two different modes. *Permissive* mode is good for debugging your configuration as it will allow MongoDB to attempt all accesses, but will log every attempt. Once you switch SELinux into *enforcing* mode, it will block any unauthorized access and possibly prevent your MongoDB instance from behaving as expected.

You can check the current mode by running `getenforce` or see a full status with `sestatus`. In order to make enforcing the default mode on system start, you will normally just need to edit the `/etc/selinux/config` file.

When MongoDB is installed via the prepackaged RPM files, there are certain standard directories used for storing data and log files:

- `/var/lib/mongo` (the data directory)

- `/var/log/mongodb` (the log directory)

The default SELinux configuration for MongoDB that is included in Red Hat Enterprise Linux 7 (and its forks) assumes these same directories, so if you chose to configure your MongoDB to store data or logs in a different location, you will have to manually update the SELinux permissions with a series of commands. For example, if you want to store your data in a new partition /data/mongodb, you would need to run the following commands to allow MongoDB to launch and function correctly:

```
semanage fcontext -a -t mongod_var_lib_t '/data/mongodb.*'
chcon -Rv -u system_u -t mongod_var_lib_t '/data/mongodb'
restorecon -R -v '/data/mongodb'
```

Similarly, to use a nonstandard port for binding, you would need to run:

```
semanage port -a -t mongod_port_t -p tcp <portnumber>
```

If SELinux prevents your MongoDB instance from starting correctly, it will log all details in a custom format into a local /var/log/audit/audit.log file. If you hit any problems when configuring your MongoDB with SELinux enforcing, there are a few tools and commands that can help explain the problem based on this audit.log.

audit2allow can help generate a new set of SELinux policies which you can introduce with a higher priority than the defaults to override these included policies.

Alternatively, running

```
sudo sealert -a /var/log/audit/audit.log
```

will activate the *setroubleshoot* client tool and usually give some useful insights and recommendations for SELinux config changes.

It's really worth going to the extra trouble to enable SELinux and get your MongoDB production instance running in enforcing mode. If possible, stick with default ports and directory paths since keeping these standards will also help new team members to onboard and simplify any later troubleshooting.

Binary monitoring

There are a few solutions designed to add an extra layer of protection to critical applications running in sensitive enterprises like banks or hospitals. These tools manipulate the binary code and replace certain operations (like memory allocation) with their own functions. The idea is to monitor and prevent certain vectors of attacks. Companies such as Imperva have tools that claim to be compatible with MongoDB, but my limited experience with these tools is that they can add instability and the extra protection promised is hard to quantify.

Certification

The ISO/IEC 27000 family of standards helps organizations keep information assets secure. ISO/IEC 27001 in particular specifies a set of best practices and details a list of security controls concerning the management of information risks.

While the 27001 Standard does not mandate specific information security controls, the framework and checklist of controls it lays out allow companies to ensure a comprehensive and continually improving model for security management.

Another popular framework is Payment Card Industry Data Security Standard (PCI DSS). Even if you are not storing credit card data, the core requirements are a good checklist of security activities.

If your data is particularly sensitive, your organization should consider certifying your security practices. MongoDB Inc.'s certifications and whitepapers for Atlas are a useful reference at `www.mongodb.com/cloud/trust`.

Checklist

In summary, here's a checklist of all the steps that should be taken to secure a MongoDB deployment:

1. Enable authentication (and create MongoDB users with the least privileges necessary to complete their use cases), and if available, use Kerberos for external authentication.

2. Secure the network infrastructure by blocking incoming connections from all but trusted IPs/networks and blocking all noncritical ports.

3. Ensure that most users to the host can only read but not modify MongoDB data or log files.

4. Configure encryption between all components (internal authentication, replication) and from clients with well-defined x.509 certificates.

5. Encrypt data at rest with filesystem encryption, or application-level encryption with a regularly rotated master key (Enterprise only).

6. Enable audit logs sent to a centralized log server (Enterprise only).

7. Redact log files to avoid leaking sensitive user data into the logs (Enterprise only).

8. Disable server-side JavaScript.

9. Enforce SELinux.

10. Remove user accounts when no longer required (i.e., when people leave the team).

11. Upgrade to any MongoDB minor releases as soon as possible to take advantage of security fixes.

12. Monitor the Security Alerts page at `www.mongodb.com/alerts` for any updates.

CHAPTER 4

Compliance and GDPR

Relying on the government to protect your privacy is like asking a peeping tom to install your window blinds.

—John Perry Barlow, cyberlibertarian, political activist, and founding member of the Electronic Frontier Foundation

Businesses that make consumer privacy a point of competitive differentiation will enjoy greater customer loyalty.

—Pierre Nanterme, Chairman and CEO of Accenture

Data privacy has become something that is not just for the lawyers anymore. At LinkedIn we call it a culture of privacy.

—Kalinda Raina, Head of Global Privacy, LinkedIn

The ability to store humongous amounts of data creates opportunities for powerful analytical insights. With the advent of new data protection regulations around the world, it also creates compliance and security risks for companies because data is often dumped into data lakes or data warehouses without proper labeling, auditing, or policy enforcement.

MongoDB offers a number of features to *ease* some of the burdens of adhering to privacy regulations such as the right to be forgotten and the right to export one's own data. Other obligations such as the requirement to notify users of a breach of their data within 72 hours will require a custom **business workflow** and **application-side preparations**.

© Nicholas Cottrell 2020

N. Cottrell, *MongoDB Topology Design*, https://doi.org/10.1007/978-1-4842-5817-0_4

General Data Protection Regulation

While many regulations, such as the European Union's General Data Protection Regulation (GDPR), appear extremely complex, they are in fact a codification of many of the industry's best practices. Despite GDPR being an EU-based law, it applies to any organization around the world that stores or processes data about EU citizens. Noncompliance penalties are steep and can reach as high as €20 million or 4% of the perpetrating organization's annual global revenue, whichever is greater. Less severe infringements still face half that penalty.[1]

In this chapter, we will address the major compliance concerns when storing structured data about users in real-world MongoDB deployments. With the correct setup, off-the-shelf MongoDB tooling can provide visibility and transparency into what data is being stored and how it is being used. MongoDB Enterprise and MongoDB Atlas include additional security and privacy features.

As the world's strictest and most comprehensive legal regulation, we will use GDPR as the basis for most of the discussion in this chapter, although we'll also explore notable differences in other related regulations in other parts of the world.

Privacy by design

When running a database, privacy laws regulate how organizations *collect*, *store*, *process*, *retain*, and *share* the personal data of EU citizens, and this applies even to foreign companies if they process or store data about EU citizens.

This chapter focuses on how MongoDB topology design can meet data protection regulations. We cover the basic requirements of most regulations and how certain MongoDB features can be used to, for example, hide certain data based on role and remove user data as part of the "right to be forgotten."

Caveats

The GDPR requires clear evidence of an organization's *ongoing* compliance efforts. This makes it necessary to constantly monitor your data processing practices and adequately address any emerging privacy and security risks to ensure that data protection processes remain effective.

---

[1]https://gdpr.eu/fines/

Disclaimer   To ensure compliance with any laws like GDPR applicable in your country or countries of business, you should review the laws directly (e.g., *GDPR (Regulation (EU) 2016/679)* and seek legal counsel to apply those laws correctly in your situation.

Data protection

At a high level, the GDPR covers the "right to be forgotten," "right to review," and the "right to be informed" about any data leaks or mishandling.

This section will look deeper at a few issues which are of particular concern to those designing, architecting or implementation data collection, storage, or processing with MongoDB.

Key concepts

Before delving into the particulars, it's important to understand some key concepts which relate to all the data protection regulations globally.

A *data controller* is an organization which collects, stores, and processes data on private individuals and other companies, known as *data subjects*. A *data processor* is an employee, contractor, or a software tool such as MongoDB or an application which performs the processing. It is up to the controller to ensure that the processor is capable of and configured to meet all the privacy and security requirements laid out by the applicable compliance laws.

For any organization with international customers, this essentially means that they need to follow the regulations for each customer's home territory. If you have EU customers in your database and you operate in the European Union, then you need to ensure your data storage meets all the GDPR requirements; otherwise, you run the risk of breaches and penalties.

Personally identifiable information

Personal data is any information related to an identifiable individual, but does not necessarily identify the individual. *Personally identifiable information* (PII), on the other hand, is any data that could potentially identify a specific individual. Table 4-1 shows examples of which types of data are personally identifiable or not.

Table 4-1. *Examples of personal data types and which are PII*

Personally identifiable information (PII)	Personal data (non-PII)
• Full name	• Device IDs
• Social security number	• IP addresses
• Driver license number	• Cookies

Definitions

There are a lot of legal terms that make up the EU regulations which are used in the following section. Table 4-2 defines the most relevant terms.

Table 4-2. *Summary of key concepts and definitions*

Term	Definition
Entity	A person, legal corporation, organization, public authority, agency, or group who controls or processes data.
Data controller	An entity who determines the **purposes** and **means** of processing personal data (this can be determined alone, or jointly with another person/company/body).
Data subject	An identified or identifiable natural person referenced by identifying data values, also known as a **user**.
Data processor (DP)	An entity responsible for processing personal data on behalf of a data controller. This person is legally responsible for any breaches. In our context, data processors can include IT team leads, application devs, DBAs, QA teams, release managers, and DevOps engineers.
Data protection officer (DPO)	A role within an organization whose responsibility is to ensure the internal application of the regulations, and protect data subjects from being adversely affected by the processing operations.
Personal data	Any information that uniquely identifies an individual (e.g., a mobile phone device ID) and that **relates to** an identifiable individual. Any data which is truly anonymous (or fully anonymized) is not included in GDPR or any other regulations covered here.

(continued)

Table 4-2. (*continued*)

Term	Definition
Identifier	Any **types** of data that separately or in combination identify an individual, such as • Name • Social security, or tax file number • Location data • Username • Birthday
Online identifier	A specific subset of identifier for online data such as • IP address • MAC (network card) address • Browser cookie
Related factor	Other details about a personal such as physical or genetic data.
Data items	The actual field **values** stored in the database about a person.

Representatives

The GDPR requires corporations to have a local representative in the EU who is legally responsible that the regulations are applied and data protections are being followed. This allows that representative to suffer legal consequences should data be misused or abused, making it easier to apply fines and penalties.

Data portability

Data portability is a relatively new requirement in the world of data protection regulations and was created in the hope of protecting consumers from *vendor lock-in*. The topic is addressed in GDPR Article 20: Right to data portability (Chapter 3).

It means that companies must be able to supply or transfer all personal data collected about their customers upon request and in a structured, machine readable format.

With good document design in MongoDB, this requirement can be quite easily met in terms of personal data. How easy it is to discover, identify, and collect this data may depend on the schema design chosen and the level of validation applied.

> **Tip**   MongoDB Compass's "Analyze Schema" functionality can be used to more easily find *identifier* fields.

Exporting any relevant documents in JavaScript Object Notation (JSON) format should be sufficient in terms of machine readability.

A MongoDB *View* (based on an *aggregation pipeline*) could be developed using `$lookup` to bring together related documents from other collections, reformat certain fields, and exclude others.

Data size

Historical data collected from customer's Internet of Things (IoT) devices is considered personal data and should be exportable. In this case, you need to be able to provide or transfer large volumes of data. Structuring and storing data in an efficient, compact way can be important for both storage and bandwidth costs.

Consider using a *storage aggregation* technique to aggregate older data into lower-precision buckets allowing generalization of long-term trends without storing exact data. For example, you might retain hourly data points for up to one month and then keep only daily averages for up to a year.

Retention of personal data

GDPR Article 13 (clause 2a) reads as follows:

> *the controller shall, at the time when personal data are obtained, provide the data subject with the following further information necessary to ensure fair and transparent processing: (a) **the period** for which the personal data will be stored...*

This clause requires that the data controller knows *the period for which the personal data will be stored* in advance and communicates that to end users. You should have at least a policy in place to timestamp data upon collection and a means to rotate it.

Automatic removal

In one approach to automating the removal of old data, each document could have a field like `dateCollected` and a *time-to-live (TTL) index* on this collection linked to that field to automatically and completely remove documents after 12 months or so.

You should be careful about batch deletions since they can have performance implications to the replication process, especially for releases before MongoDB 4.0. A large batch of operations all occurring in the same few seconds can overwhelm the I/O and stall other operations momentarily. Ensure that the date values are granular enough to avoid this (a minute-level granularity usually works well). Also, be careful when importing or migrating data into MongoDB that you don't set the date field of a large number of documents to the same single placeholder date or to the timestamp that the import processes started. This can stall replication as described earlier if the TTL index suddenly kicks in 12 months later.

In Listing 4-1 we see message logs stored with date at the minute granularity level, and a time-to-live index which will automatically purge them after one year (365 days). Depending on the load of the system, this should create sufficiently small batches to avoid risking stalls.

Listing 4-1. Time-to-live index to delete data after one year

```
db.msglog.insertOne(
  { from: "nic", to: "sophie",
    createDate: ISODate("2019-11-04T20:55"),
    msg: "What's for dessert?" });
db.msglog.createIndex(
  { "createDate": 1 },
  { expireAfterSeconds: 365*24*3600 } )
```

Custom redaction

Another option for purging personal data is to use a `cron` job to initiate a more fine-grained or custom cleanup of older personal data. For example, you could use `$unset` update command to delete certain fields from documents after a predefined time period (see Listing 4-2).

> **Note**   MongoDB's Realm serverless platform includes "Scheduled Triggers" which allow arbitrary JavaScript functions to purge, trim, or aggregate documents at predefined intervals.

The code in Listing 4-2 performs a sort of "rolling redaction" of collected data, purging *PII* fields but leaving other fields in place that can still be data-mined later for other trends and correlations without risking exposure of stored personal data.

Listing 4-2. Unset certain metadata when it is no longer necessary

```
db.msglog.insertOne(
  { from: "nic", to: "sophie",
    createDate: ISODate("2019-11-04T20:55"),
    msg: "What's for dessert?",
    metadata: {
      deviceId: "34-A4-8C-71",
      deviceName: "iPhone XS",
      ip: "123.45.67.89",
      gps: { lat: 48.86, long: 2.349 }
  });
db.msglog.update(
    { _id: ObjectId(1234...) },
    { $unset: {metadata: "" } )
```

Right to be forgotten

Another common component of most data compliance regulations globally is a right for users to demand deletion of all data collected about them. This includes many of the same technical problems of data discovery for data portability compliance. The major difference is that data needs to be completely destroyed rather than just exported. For full compliance, user data in backups should also be purged or backup retention for personal data limited to a very short time span.

Note   MongoDB's field-level encryption support allows personal data to be encrypted with per-user keys. Deleting a user's key effectively destroys access to that data in the live database as well as all backups and copies. See the "*Design recommendations*" section for more details.

Product guarantees

In some cases, you might still need to retain some personal data associated with orders (e.g., first and last name, billing address). This data is often required for audit purposes and warrantee requirements (e.g., returns, or product recalls).

Avoid dated collections

Some architectures use an antipattern with multiple collections for the same type of data, appended with a date suffix. For example, older messages are moved into a monthly collection after 30 days. This produces databases with huge numbers of collections like:

```
user_messages
user_messages_201909
user_messages_201910
user_messages_201911
```

Not only does this approach make it harder to perform aggregations of historical data, but a large number of collections requires a significant memory overhead just to manage file handles for the underlying data files inside the operating system.

Data flows

GDPR Article 45 (clause 1) introduces a concept we will refer to as *data flows*:

> ***A transfer of personal data to a third country*** *or an international organisation **may take place** where the [European] Commission has decided that the third country, a territory or one or more specified sectors within that third country, or the international organisation in question **ensures an adequate level of protection**.*

One of the important distinctions made by GDPR is the difference between data transits and data transfers. A *data transit* is the transmission of a copy of data on a temporary basis for processing and can be thought of as "data in motion." A *data transfer*, on the other hand, is the permanent relocation of persistent data storage to another physical location and includes backups.

As you can imagine, data transfer has an even higher burden in terms of data protection and is covered in the section on *"Data storage."*

Processing data

GDPR Article 6 titled "Lawfulness of processing" allows a sharded cluster with geolocated personal data to *temporarily* copy some documents with personal data to another shard node for analytics processing, such as in an aggregation pipeline. However, this only applies if that remote location is in a preapproved location. If, for example, you have EU customer data and a cluster with physical hosts in Russia, then it would be a violation to even transit data there for processing (see Figure 4-1).

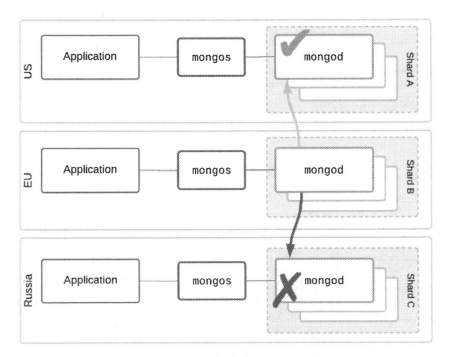

Figure 4-1. *EU data may be processed temporarily in the United States but not in Russia*

To be safe, you can configure your deployment with `mongos` routers and applications in each country and perform any necessary processing locally. This will be discussed in more detail in Chapter 8 on special configurations and Chapters 10 and 11 on advanced and extreme sharding.

End-to-end data encryption

In all cases, GDPR requires that data is communicated in a secure manner, for example, using a recent TLS encryption version with a certificate authority to prevent man-in-the-middle attacks.

Data storage

The security and management of personal data storage is a major consideration in most regulations around the world. This section examines some techniques to keep data safe once stored or by obfuscating it during collection.

Data mapping

Most of the global regulations require the *data protection officer* (DPO) to not only know what data is stored but also **where** it is stored. For example, if you are storing personal data on a sharded cluster, the DPO must be aware of how the shard key influences on which hosts and data centers that data is stored.

This requirement also means that the *data controller* must be able to track data inside backups and be able to confirm compliance even in this data (e.g., the "right to be forgotten").

It is important to maintain up-to-date documentation of data schema and know which collections and fields contain personal data, what format it is in, which documents need to be purged after a certain period, and which data should be pseudonymized/anonymized after certain time.

Here again, controllers can use tools like MongoDB Compass for data exploration and schema discovery. It's also important to identify invalid data values since those may accidentally cause personal data to be stored in an unexpected location, when those fields form part of the shard key, for example.

Auditing changes

MongoDB Enterprise edition supports a number of auditing features that can be crucial to guaranteeing that there has not been any unauthorized data access, nor changes to user access privileges. The auditing subsystem will record any such changes to separate logs files and allows streaming these logs to a secure remote location to prevent tampering.

Using Ops Manager (available with MongoDB Enterprise Advanced), data controllers can be automatically and instantly alerted whenever certain changes are made to a database configuration. This can be critical for demonstrating to regulation authorities that all possible measures are being taken to ensure secure handling of personal data.

Validation

MongoDB's support for *JSON Schema* allows database administrators to specify complex schema rules for documents in each collection. By requiring certain identifiers to be stored in a specific format (i.e., all social security numbers are stored in the same string format and not partly as integers), it ensures that data is properly discoverable should there ever be a request for removal, or the need to notify users about a data breach.

Schema validation can be configured just as a warning, or to block inserts and update operations which would fail. Validation will not apply to preexisting documents. The $jsonSchema query operator can be used to find any documents failing to match recently added schema validation rules.

Pseudonymization

Pseudonymized data is any data that has been obfuscated with original values maintained in a separate lookup table, allowing values to be restored to its original state and for individuals to be reidentified.

By contrast, *anonymized data* randomly substitutes values with realistic and similar data of the same type but without any correlations, meaning that data can never be restored to its original state.

Pseudonymization is an issue in, for example, patient-related data that has to be passed on securely between clinical centers, each with separate databases. Certain regulations require special handling of pseudonymized data, whereas fully anonymized data is usually exempt from data protection regulations.

In MongoDB, it's possible to use Views (based on an *aggregation pipeline*) to replace all instances of an identifying unique key value (such as a social security number) with an artificial identifier. This still allows certain analytics such as grouping and cross-collection of references across an entire database without exposing the original value.

When using MongoDB as a source for data analysis or analytics, another approach during ingestion is to replace the PII with pseudonyms at "import time" (see Figure 4-2), meaning that identifiable data is never inserted into the database in the first place.

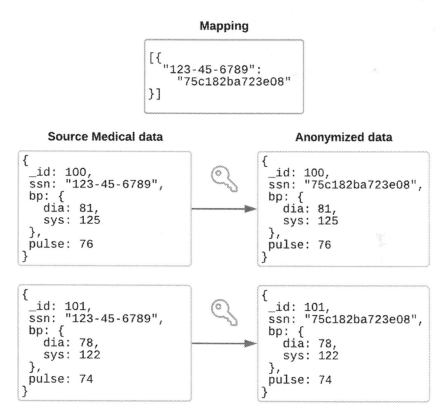

Mapping

```
[{
    "123-45-6789":
        "75c182ba723e08"
}]
```

Source Medical data

```
{
  _id: 100,
  ssn: "123-45-6789",
  bp: {
    dia: 81,
    sys: 125
  },
  pulse: 76
}
```

```
{
  _id: 101,
  ssn: "123-45-6789",
  bp: {
    dia: 78,
    sys: 122
  },
  pulse: 74
}
```

Anonymized data

```
{
  _id: 100,
  ssn: "75c182ba723e08",
  bp: {
    dia: 81,
    sys: 125
  },
  pulse: 76
}
```

```
{
  _id: 101,
  ssn: "75c182ba723e08",
  bp: {
    dia: 78,
    sys: 122
  },
  pulse: 74
}
```

Figure 4-2. *Sensitive data is anonymized but allows recovery*

A detailed solution to this problem will be presented in the "Views" section later in this chapter.

Generalizing data

Another approach to avoid storing personal data in the first place is to *generalize data* during insertion into the database. For example, when setting the birthdate field, record only the birth year, for postcode only store the first few digits, and zero out the others to keep general information for bucketing purposes but without being able to track back to original users.

The same approach can be used when storing GPS locations. Alternatively, some random "noise" can be added to the value, like certain major handset vendors do when collecting metrics on mobile device usage. By changing the value slightly to a similar and still valid value, analytics can still be performed without violating user privacy.

Encryption at rest

Part of the generally accepted requirements for data protection is to ensure that data is encrypted while stored on disk so that even if files are somehow copied, their contents cannot be accessed.

MongoDB allows native encryption of all data files using the WiredTiger storage engine. Alternatively, you could use encryption functionality provided at the storage layer, for example, via encrypted LVM (Logical Volume Manager) on Linux, or using AWS's encrypted EBS (Elastic Block Store) volumes.

More details about encryption options are covered in Chapter 3.

Backups

Another critical consideration for designing a compliant MongoDB cluster is how and where the backups will be stored. At the time of writing, the European Union's GDPR is the strictest global regulation, so the simplest approach is to store all backups in Europe. This way you can automate a simple nightly mongodump for your replica set or use MongoDB's enterprise-level *Ops Manager* tool to create continuous backups of your sharded cluster into special backup nodes with storage on servers physically located inside the European Union. MongoDB's hosted *Atlas* service also allows you to choose the storage location of continuous backup data, to meet your particular requirements.

As other laws come into effect such as the Personal Information Protection and Electronic Documents Act (PIPEDA) in Canada and California's new legislation, it will become more difficult to meet all regulations simultaneously. Global clusters (explained in Chapter 6) are a special type of sharded cluster where users' data is stored close to their physical location usually to minimize latency. This approach also means that their data can be stored in the same country (or legislative zone) making it much easier to back up the data in compliance (see Figure 4-3)

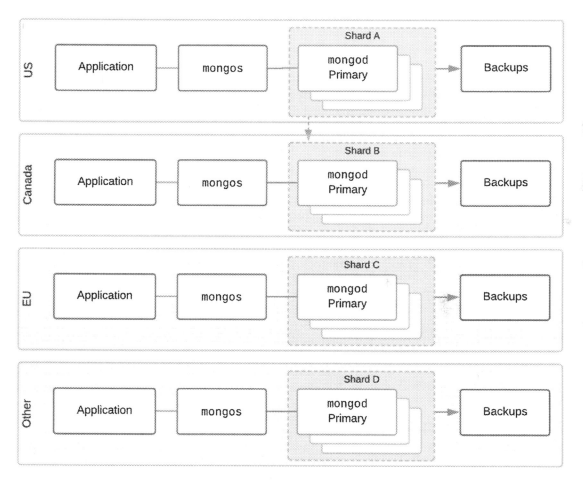

Figure 4-3. *A sharded cluster with backups of each shard stored "locally"*

Regulations around the world

The European Union's GDPR is by far the most well-known and widely discussed data protection regulation that should concern us as database architects and administrators. There are many other regulations coming online which may also be of concern, depending on the location of your customers, your business, and your industry.

One common factor in many of the new privacy laws is the concept that the entity which controls personal data must be able to legally justify the purpose of collecting the data in the first place. In our context, this means that we shouldn't be collecting superfluous metadata that isn't required by the service being offered.

US healthcare

The *Health Insurance Portability and Accountability Act* (HIPAA) is a regulation which targets the US healthcare data industry. The act covers genetic data which is sometimes impossible to depersonalize since the exact values are required for research but also identify the individual. In this case, encryption of the data with secure external keys is critical.

California

The California Consumer Privacy Act (CCPA) of 2018 took effect on January 1, 2020, and covers the rights of consumers for corporations conducting business in the State of California and which holds data on more than 50,000 people. This set of regulations shares many of the same goals as GDPR and covers many of the same issues.

Although the CCPA is **not** modeled after or structured the same way as the GDPR, it has all the same best practices.

India

At the time of writing, India is in the process of developing their own version of GDPR including regulations for the right to access and correct data, the right to portability (i.e., export one's own data), and the right to be forgotten. Currently, its powers are less extreme compared to GDPR.

However, the proposed law does impose strict **data localization** rules, mandating both the storage and processing of personal data physically inside India. This is in stark contrast to GDPR which allows temporary *transit* of data outside of the EU for processing as long as conditions (such as secure encrypted communication) are met.

This localization requirement would be satisfied by keeping a shard reserved for Indian customer data with hosts in an Indian data center. This approach will be discussed further at the end of this chapter and in Chapter 11 on extreme sharding.

If India's law finally only requires a "mirror" copy of an entity's personal data to be kept on a server physically in India, then this requirement is easily satisfied with a replica set node in an Indian data center.

Canada

The Personal Information Protection and Electronic Documents Act (PIPEDA) and the Privacy Act that govern Canada cover many of the same general rights as GDPR but with less specificity.

It's important to note, however, that many *individual provinces* in Canada have substantial privacy regulations of their own which are broadly similar to but tend to extend and further complicate the national-level regulations.

China

China has the most Internet users in the world but at the time of writing does not yet have single comprehensive data protection *regulation*.

In March 2018, China's Standard's Committee TC260 issued a national *standard*, the "Personal Information Security Specification," which provides guidance on the collection, storage, use, sharing, transfer, and disclosure of personal information.

This standard does not yet result in legal or financial consequences, but national legislation is likely to arrive shortly which may require explicit consent for using and processing user data. There appears to be no automatic provisions for processing as a normal part of a contract between company and customer, so *consent* will be stricter than GDPR.

In terms of MongoDB, you may need to at least maintain an array of different processing use cases for each user in the system to be able to track who has given consent for which activities.

Russia

Since Russia has not been short-listed as a country offering an adequate level of data protection under GDPR, it is not automatically allowed to transit EU data to Russia for even temporary processing. In terms of MongoDB, it is advisable to both store and process data inside the EU, or keep separate shards for EU and Russian personal data as discussed in later chapters.

Design recommendations

In this section we will cover some approaches that have been shown to best address compliance concerns during the application design phase.

Field-level encryption

One of the new security features of MongoDB 4.2 is client-side field-level encryption (FLE). With support added to the official drivers, this allows applications to encrypt certain fields and subdocuments with an external key **prior** to sending the data over the wire. The effect is that critical or sensitive user data is available only to the application and never reaches the database unencrypted. Should an intruder somehow access the live data inside a running mongod process (such as the exploits known as *Meltdown* and *Spectre*), the field values would still be encrypted.

The application interfaces with an *external key store* (not part of MongoDB) to securely manage these keys and adds another level of security but also complexity. This approach has the added benefit that backups via mongodump or Ops Manager backups are also encrypted and secure.

The keys can be created not only at the database or collection level but even on a per-user, per-document basis. This makes it easier to permanently erase user data from both the live database and also *all backups*.

In Figure 4-4 we can see an Application retrieving a per-user key for extracting the data subdocument from a user profile. This key will be needed for any operation on the document for encrypted values. This means that any sort of server-side aggregations on this data field (or its subfields) will not be possible since they are essentially seen as binary data by the MongoDB query engine.

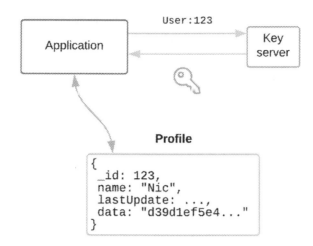

Figure 4-4. *The application encrypts the data subdocument*

When using *deterministic encryption*, the client can perform equality queries on encrypted field values. On the other hand, *randomized encryption* provides stronger confidentiality but limits operations on encrypted fields during queries.

By discarding the old key for a particular user, it becomes virtually impossible to ever decode those encrypted values. As you can see, this can become a very convenient way to ensure GDPR and similar compliance regulations' "right to be forgotten" requirements since it instantly and permanently locks all encrypted values in both the live database and all backups.

Views

MongoDB allows us to build a *View* defined as a multistage aggregation pipeline. By leveraging a set of different operators, we can transform all documents in a collection in a standard way, creating a new virtual collection which can be granted broader access within an organization while the original collection with full data values accessible only by a trusted few user accounts.

In **Listing 4-3**, we see a view that takes both a "vertical" and "horizontal" subset of the data available in this collection. The aggregation pipeline first calculate customers' ages from their birthdates, then divides by the number of milliseconds in a year to get the age in years.

The resulting view only includes documents for study participants who are over 18 and excludes their name, social security number, birthday, and exact street address. These views leave fields like `address.postcode` and `address.state` so that analytics could still be performed with grouping or visualizations based on postcode without any identifiable data possible to be extracted or restored.

Listing 4-3. View definition excluding certain personal data

```
db.createView(
  "participants_adults_nonpersonal",
  "participants",
  [ { $addFields: {
        age: {
          $divide: [{
            $subtract: [new Date(), "$birthdate"]
          },
          365.25 * 24 * 60 * 60 * 1000]
        }
     }},
   { $match: { age: { $gt: 18 }}},
   { $project: {
       name: 0, ssn: 0, birthdate: 0,
         "address.street": 0, age: 0
     }}
  ])
```

The `$redact` aggregation pipeline stage is another powerful option that can be used in a view to conditionally prune fields from documents based on nesting depth or the value of other fields in the same document.

Separate permissions

The view itself is exposed as if it were a read-only collection. *Role-based access controls* (RBAC) mean that an individual user or a group can be granted read privileges to a view, but have no access to the underlying source collection that contains the personal data. The view can safely be shared with a wider audience to perform analytics or reporting without risking the exposure of sensitive information.

For example, in a medical study you could grant a role called `controller` with read access to the original `participants` collection so that only trusted users can see the full data. In Listing 4-4, we see that another role called `researcher` could be granted read access to only the derived view `participants_adults_nonpersonal`. These researchers can never see identifying values, but can still manipulate the data for their analysis.

Listing 4-4. Custom role and user who can query this view only

```
use admin;
db.createRole({
    role  : "researcher",
    privileges : [
      {
        resource : {
            db : "app1",
            collection : " participants_adults_nonpersonal" },
        actions  : [ "find" ]
      }
    ],
      roles : []
    })

db.createUser({
  user : "nic",
  pwd : "securepassword",
  roles : ["researcher "] }
)
```

Data leaks

There are a few other potential sources of personal data leaking out of the database into other locations.

Sharding

In a sharded cluster, personal data is stored on the shard nodes. Using geolocated sharding, you can control where that data goes. In such cases, you should avoid choosing a shard key that includes user data fields such as a social security number, for example, `{country: 1, ssn: 1}`. In this case, the values will form part of the chunk boundaries and will also be recorded in the sharded cluster's `config` database which may physically reside in another jurisdiction.

Logging

By default, MongoDB will log any queries that take longer than 100ms to complete. When logging a query, the complete query including values is recorded in the log allowing for convenient reproduction and optimization. However, when queries are on personal data fields, these will also be logged to a potentially insecure log file.

In order to avoid these leaks (in exchange for a small performance hit), it's possible to tell MongoDB to redact any field values from the logs by setting `security.redactClientLogData: true` in the node configuration file.

Once this configuration parameter is set, an insert on a document like `{ "name" : "Nic", "SSN" : "123-45-6789" }` would result in a log line as shown in Listing 4-5.

Listing 4-5. Log output with redaction showing all client values as hashes

```
2019-10-07T11:10:02.321+0200 I COMMAND [conn2] command test.clients
appName: "MongoDB Shell" command:
insert {
  insert: "###", ordered: "###",
  lsid: { id: "###" }, $db: "###" }
  ninserted:1 keysInserted:1 numYields:0 reslen:45
  locks:{ ... }
```

Minimize vulnerabilities

It is tempting to imagine security breaches as an external hacker gaining access to a database through a security vulnerability in a network infrastructure or some unpatched software. In contrast, some data breaches can be as simple as improperly disposing of a hard drive or could be caused by an insider taking an unauthorized copy of personal data and selling it to a third party.

Remember to properly destroy storage devices, limit access to all databases, and remove access as soon as someone leaves the organization.

Summary

Every application that uses a database to store personal data should employ *privacy by design*. To help ensure that your MongoDB database meets or exceeds the requirements for data protection regulations around the world, Table 4-3 lists the major issues you need to consider.

Table 4-3. *A summary of GDPR problems and solutions with MongoDB*

Requirement	Solution
Lawful and transparent	Ask permission, explain what data is stored, and only store personal data required for the service provided. Record what permission each user has given.
Integrity and confidentiality	Secure access to the live databases with user access controls (e.g., LDAP authorization), x509 certificates, encrypted TLS 1.2+ connections, firewalls, encryption at rest, restricted access to hosts, encrypted network storage and backups, and even field-level encryption. Enable auditing on MongoDB to monitor any changes in user permissions. Enable alerts for monitoring any important changes so data controllers are immediately aware of any concerns. Notify both authorities and users directly if any breaches are detected.
Limit to purpose	Ensure data stored is in scope for the permissions given; data should be pseudonymized or anonymized, or purged completely.
Limit to time	Data should not be kept longer than necessary and not longer than was communicated to users. Use TTL indexes for live data and rolling removal of backups of personal data.
Minimize data stored	When data is no longer useful for the service provided, it should be trimmed and only required data kept (i.e., to track purchases for tax auditing, or guarantees).
Data accuracy	You have a limited window to update, correct, and deliver personal data from the subject upon request, so it's better to keep data well-structured and in one logical location.

(continued)

Table 4-3. (*continued*)

Requirement	Solution
Protect data in transit	Encrypt communication between MongoDB members and with client applications (via official drivers) and TLS certificates.
Manage data location	Use country-level sharding to keep personal data and associated backups inside the country of origin.
Protect data at rest	Encrypt data inside the storage engine, or encrypt the entire filesystem.
Right to be forgotten	Ensure that both the live database and backups are purged. Consider field-level encryption with individual keys per-user.
Limit sensitive information to authorized users	Enable authentication and authorization using SCRAM, Kerberos, LDAP, etc. Use views to redact sensitive fields; skip certain individual's data based on criteria like age, country of residence, etc. Define access controls to limit access to source collections to a few trusted users.

CHAPTER 5

Basic Topologies

This chapter walks through common deployment topologies depending on the number of data centers available. We address the limitations of each topology and how to best configure nodes and backups to optimize availability.

Introduction

Historically, the first experience that most people have with MongoDB is running it locally. You can very easily download MongoDB for free and install it on your local PC or Mac. With the Mongo shell, a visual tool like Compass or Studio 3T, or through some programming UI, you can be writing and reading data from a MongoDB server in minutes.

Local MongoDB instances are fantastic for developers and researchers who want to learn or run experiments, but not suitable for any sort of production workloads. As we've already discussed, one key strength of MongoDB is its distributed nature. The real revolution compared to MySQL or other open source databases is how easily and flexibly MongoDB can be scaled out to suit your use case.

If you are servicing an internal application, to internal customers in a single location, then a cluster in a single physical location might be just fine. If, by contrast, you're building a startup with a global audience, you want to be able to have their data as close as possible to reduce latency and meet compliance obligations (Chapter 4).

Table 5-1 shows a quick overview of different environments and benefits of increasing the number of data centers. Each row adds additional benefits over the row above.

© Nicholas Cottrell 2020
N. Cottrell, *MongoDB Topology Design*, https://doi.org/10.1007/978-1-4842-5817-0_5

Table 5-1. *A summary of topologies and use cases*

Environment	Benefits
Single standalone server	Quick start for prototyping, development, and simple testing.
Replica set, One data center	Now any single server can fail without the loss of data nor any downtime.
Two data centers	Now an entire data center can be lost permanently without loss of data. Manual intervention required to restore writes.
Two data centers (plus cloud arbiter)	Now an entire data center can be lost without any application downtime, and writes are still possible.
Three data centers	Now an entire data center can be lost and the application can continue writing to a majority of nodes, so that data rollbacks can never occur.
Geolocated data centers	Now using geolocalized sharding, data can be stored close to users to reduce latency and comply with data protection regulations.

Co-locating nodes

Before diving into details, it's also important to understand the drawbacks of co-locating multiple nodes on a single host for production uses. In some circumstances, due to budget or administrative limitations, it may be tempting to install multiple MongoDB components on a single host or VM. In a sharded cluster, you might plan to install a config server node on the same host as a shard member, or with a `mongos` router.

Installing multiple components onto a single host is generally a bad idea as it complicates the configuration (several components share the same hostname but with different ports) and can make it harder to quickly comprehend logs and diagnostic data.

Another issue is with the WiredTiger cache for data-bearing nodes. By default, this special cache reserves almost half the host's RAM. With two nodes on one host, no RAM is left for filesystem cache or the operating system.

If you must co-locate nodes, you will need to at least set the `storage.wiredTiger.engineConfig.cacheSizeGB` configuration option. The preferred approach is to instead use a separate VM for each node.

Communications between components

Since MongoDB is intended as a distributed system, the communication between components is a critical issue when planning a deployment.

Connections and heartbeats

All components in a MongoDB cluster need to be able to communicate with all others, to synchronize data, to monitor health and availability, and to react to changes. To facilitate this communication, each node, application (via the driver), and `mongos` router opens at least one connection to every other component in its set to send regular heartbeat messages back and forth. Should one of these heartbeats be delayed, it means that a component may be under extremely heavy load. If heartbeats are missed completely, this may indicate that the other member is unavailable either due to a load or a network issue. If a **primary** node misses a heartbeat, a failure mechanism is then triggered with timers counting down until an election is called to elect a replacement.

Routing

MongoDB supports a wide range of possible deployment topologies. To achieve this there are a number of different settings and mechanisms to automate routing of queries to maximize stability and performance through a special type of *load balancing*.

Discovery

The *server discovery and monitoring* (SDAM) specification defines how all official application drivers connect to and monitor complex MongoDB deployments. It specifies how drivers adapt to changes in the deployment such as nodes going offline, primaries stepping down, and network errors. It helps ensure that all drivers (no matter the programming language) will react in a consistent, predictable manner.

Server selection algorithm

Another specification is the *server selection algorithm* (SSA) which describes a sort of intelligent load balancing. The SSA is included in the driver specification and is followed by all official MongoDB drivers.

This algorithm controls how the driver (inside the application space) decides where to route an operation to your MongoDB deployment. When working with a replica set, this algorithm decides whether a query is sent to the primary or a secondary. When communicating with a sharded cluster, it will decide which of multiple mongos nodes will be used.

Figure 5-1 shows the application in DC1 might use either mongos in the same DC, but will not use the mongos in DC2 as the latency is too high. The mongos in DC1 will route queries to the primary or the secondary in DC1 (but not in DC2) depending on the read preference requested.

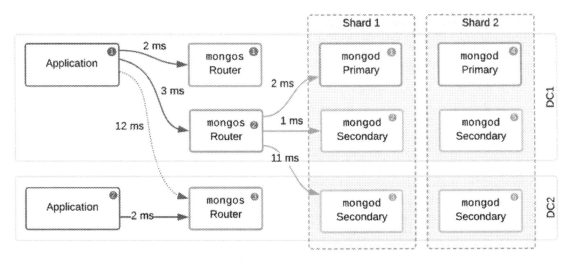

Figure 5-1. *Server selection in a sharded cluster*

Shard routers (mongos)

Any sharded cluster should contain multiple mongos router nodes and **all** should be listed in the application's *connection URI string* (since they are intentionally not automatically discovered).

The primary purpose of multiple nodes is to allow failover should one router node fail completely. However, an automatic *performance* mechanism inside the driver is also active. This mechanism monitors the *round-trip time* (RTT) latency of the pool of mongoses. It determines a "window" of acceptable latencies based on the best of the mongos nodes available. The driver will then route queries to any of the mongoses within this latency window, effectively distributing the workload between them. This distribution can be critical during periods of exceptional load to ensure that no single mongos is overloaded.

> **Tip**   If you want to force an application to distribute load equally across all mongoses, even those with higher latency, then set a high value for `localThresholdMS` in the connection string.

Replica set node selection

According to best practices, your replica set nodes should be distributed over multiple data centers, making the latency of geographically close nodes potentially very different to distant ones. Since writes will always go to the primary, you could use a higher `priority` (in the replica set configuration) to make the primary be elected in the same DC as your application servers.

Although not a default behavior, reads can be performed against secondaries also. This is where some clever design can allow for scalable solutions in certain cases. MongoDB drivers support an array of read preferences as outlined in Table 5-2.

Table 5-2. *Replica set read preferences*

Preference	Notes
primary (default)	All read operations are sent to the primary node.
secondary	All read operations are sent to secondary nodes. If there is currently only a primary available and no secondaries, these operations will stall. Use `secondaryPreferred` instead.
nearest	The driver will communicate with any nodes (primary or secondary) which fall within the lowest round-trip time (RTT) window.
primaryPreferred	The driver will read from the primary whenever possible, but will fall back to a secondary node if there is no primary available. This is recommended for applications which need to function during *network partitions*.
secondaryPreferred	The driver will read from secondaries whenever possible, but will read from a primary if no secondaries are available. This is a more robust choice than `secondary`.

For all read preference options except `primary,` there is the option for the driver to choose among several nodes, and in all cases a `maxStalenessSeconds` or *tag set* can be provided to control the selection.

By specifying an explicit `maxStalenessSeconds` in the Connection URI, the driver will exclude any nodes whose *replication lag* is longer than this value. This allows clients to safely read from secondaries and despite knowing that they will be reading stale data, the documents returned will be at worst only a few seconds behind the primary.

Tag sets

Specifying *tag sets* on particular nodes can be used (i) to specify particular physical locations for rudimentary geographical targeting within replica sets or (ii) to control specific read workflows when reading from secondary.

You could, for example, send all analytics workloads to a third faraway data center (DC2) with high latency leaving the closer nodes in DC1-a and DC1-b to share the normal read workload. Figure 5-2 shows that while writes will always go to the primary, read operations will go the DC2 when the application specifies a tag set with {`use: "analytics"`}.

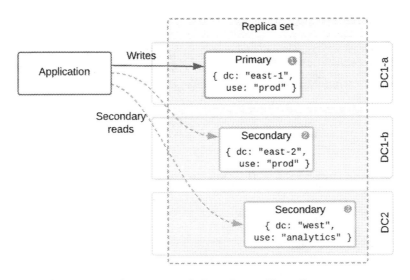

Figure 5-2. *A replica set with tag sets defined on all nodes*

Tags can be defined and changed using the `rs.reconfig(...)` method and passing an updated configuration document such as the one in Listing 5-1.

Listing 5-1. Replica set config with region and usage tags

```
{
    "_id" : "myRS",
    ...
    "members" : [
        { "_id" : 0, "host" : "mongodb0.bigbank.local:27017", ...,
            "tags": { "dc": "east-1", "use": "prod" }, ... },
        { "_id" : 1, "host" : "mongodb1.bigbank.local:27017", ...,
            "tags": { "dc": "east-2", "use": "prod" }, ... },
        { "_id" : 2, "host" : "mongodb2.bigbank.local:27017", ...,
            "tags": { "dc": "west", "use": "analytics" }, ... }
    ],
    ...
}
```

To actually use these tags, the application will need to set **read preferences tags** in a specific order for the driver to parse and use. In Listings 5-1 and 5-2, we see an example that targets node `mongodb2.bigbank.local:27017` since that is the only node with a matching use tag. If multiple tags are sent by the application, each one will be attempted in order with the most overlapping chosen first.

Listing 5-2. Aggregation operation using tags to target an analytics secondary

```
db.transactions.aggregate([...]).readPref( "secondaryPreferred",
    [ { "use": " analytics " } ] )
```

Write concerns

While writes will always be routed to the primary node, when using a custom *write concern* (WC), the driver will wait for other nodes to acknowledge that the write has been persisted before reporting a success to the application. For example, a write concern of 2 will require the primary and at least one secondary to have replicated the write before moving on. This allows the application to choose a *custom durability* for each use case and maximize performance without sacrificing the required durability. MongoDB drivers default to a WC of 1, but a WC of `majority` is recommended for all production use cases.

In Figure 5-3 we see the primary send the **Ack** back to the application as soon as one secondary (3) has replicated the oplog entry. The other secondary (2) will replicate as soon as possible, but the application will not wait for it.

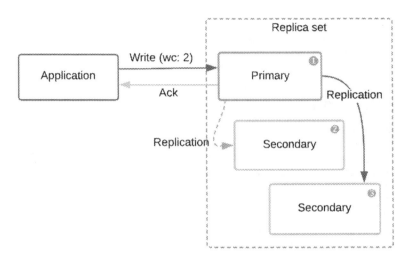

Figure 5-3. *Write concern: 2 requires 2 nodes to acknowledge the change*

Journaling

An additional option, j, allows the application to request the server to wait until the write operation has been written to the *on-disk journal*. If this is set to false, the write is acknowledged back to the application as soon as the change is applied in memory, but not necessarily written to disk. When false, the application may get a **slightly faster** response, but risk **losing the write** completely should the host suddenly fail. The default behavior when j is unspecified will depend on the write concern used and may change between versions.

Warning   For production deployments, you should never set {j: false}. The journal write is usually very fast and can be optimized further by placing it on its own separate storage volume.

Timeouts

You can optionally set a wtimeout time limit in milliseconds for the write concern. If the timeout is exceeded (due to high replication lag, for example), the acknowledgment will be reported back to the application as **failed**. The operation is **not** terminated automatically after this timeout, however, and may eventually succeed on the server side.

This can add significant confusion and complexity to application logic since developers may assume the data is lost. It is better to **avoid** this option and use retryable reads and writes instead (discussed later).

Custom durability

The application can combine **write concern** with **tag sets** to control which nodes should be acknowledging the write. This can be used to control replication lag on certain nodes (i.e., make one secondary have no effective lag at any time) or to ensure that two nodes in *different data centers* persist every write.

This can be particularly important for configurations with nodes in multiple regions (shown in Figure 5-4). Here, we assume that DC1-a and DC1-b are two buildings in the same city, and DC2 is in a different city. Since *node 2* is in the same region as the primary, it will have lower latency and will normally replicate faster. In times of network pressure or network instability, you may get an application with write concern 2 returning a success to the application, but the remote data center lags several minutes behind in its replication. Should the entire DC1 region fail together, those last several minutes of writes will have been lost.

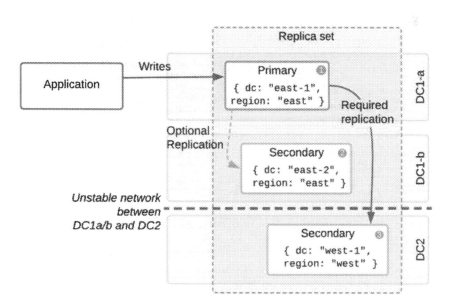

Figure 5-4. *Unstable network leads to distant nodes with unacceptable lag*

To ensure that the write is replicated to at least two separate regions, we can define a **custom** write concern level called `multi_dc` which requires nodes with two different values for the tag `region`:

```
conf = rs.conf();
conf.settings = {
  getLastErrorModes: { multi_dc : { "region": 2 } }
};
rs.reconfig(conf);
```

Then the application can use this custom `multi_dc` write concern for important inserts or updates to force updates in both regions:

```
db.collection.update( { _id: 123, status: "Important" },
  { writeConcern: { w: "multi_dc" } } )
```

In this example, it doesn't matter which of the three nodes is primary at the time, we will always replicate the change to both DC1 and DC2.

Read concerns

A related concept is *read concern* which allows you to control the consistency and isolation of read operations from replica sets and shards. For example, a system exclusively using write concern `majority`, together with a read concern of `majority`, can be sure that the data returned has been acknowledged by a majority of the replica set members. In other words, the documents returned by the read operation are durable, even in the event of any member failure.

Single data center

In a single data center topology, we have limited options, but we can maximize availability by building our replica sets with more than three members. For example, we might build our replica sets using seven members.

We can add extra safeguards by putting each node on its own physical host. Each node's host should be put on its own rack preferably on a different power circuit, with separate backup power.

> **Warning**   Nodes on different VMs but on the same underlying VM host will fail together if a single hardware failure occurs on the VM host.

Each physical host should have **redundant networking**. This could be achieved with "*network bonding*" (also known as *link aggregation*). There are many different modes available, including a round-robin balancer which provides load balancing and Active-Backup which provides only fault tolerance. In most modern Linux flavors, this can be enabled with `modprobe` and on Debian with `ifenslave`. You should confirm with your network administrator to ensure that your network switches have support for network bonding.

Avoid using **shared network storage** solutions for the data volumes on MongoDB nodes. This approach means that the data for all replica set members is actually storage on the same storage solution. It's safer to use fast storage like NVMe drives, local to each host.

Backups should be taken as often as possible and stored on a secure cloud provider in an encrypted state. If using MongoDB Enterprise, Ops Manager can provide continuous backup with point-in-time restores.

You should regularly test **restoring** from backups, to confirm the workflow and ensure that a cluster can be restored within the recovery time objective (RTO).

In general, however, a single data center is too risky for any production use cases. Regional power failure will always cause downtime, and a fire could easily cause complete data loss.

Two data centers

With two data centers, you have the opportunity to keep at least one data-bearing node in each data center. In **Figure 5-5,** we see a PSS or PS|S (Primary–Secondary–Secondary) topology distributed over two data centers. Now in case of a complete data center failure, there is a complete up-to-date copy of the entire database.

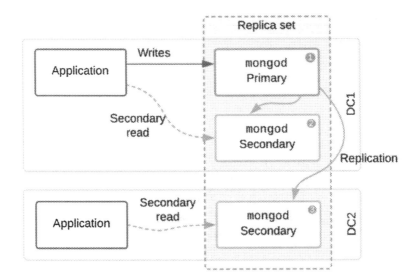

Figure 5-5. *Best 2-data center configuration*

In this configuration, if DC2 fails completely, DC1 maintains a majority of nodes and can continue to host the primary. However, should DC1 fail, only one of three nodes is left, and the remaining node in DC2 cannot elect itself primary and accept writes. Since it doesn't know if there is simply a *network partition* and there is already a primary in DC1, it must remain a secondary. The application in DC2 can still read the stale data, but will time out if attempting any writes.

Two data centers (plus cloud arbiter)

If you have access to only two data centers for storing production data, you could use a remote arbiter on a cloud provider as an impartial voter and to avoid "split-brain" in the cluster.

If a cloud provider is not allowed under your security policy, a third private data center in a remote location could be used, even if it is normally not suitable for hosting data-bearing nodes due to lower capacity or high latency.

As we discussed in Chapter 1, an arbiter doesn't replicate or store any user data. As such, it has very low network bandwidth and storage requirements, and it not a risk for data protection regulations (Chapter 4). Its sole purpose is to participate in elections by determining which data-bearing data centers are currently reachable from the rest of the network.

One major problem with a so-called PSA (Primary–Secondary–Arbiter) configuration is that your application cannot enable majority writes and continue with a data center failure (see Figure 5-6). If either data center is unavailable, only one data-bearing node remains and majority writes will just time out until the DC is restored.

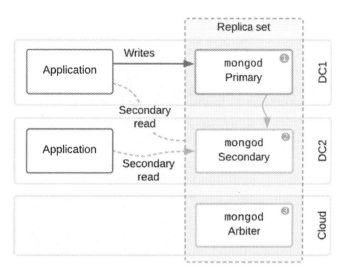

Figure 5-6. *An arbiter in the cloud but without safe majority writes*

Warning   Arbiters introduce a number of undesirable edge cases when data-bearing nodes are down (particularly for read concern `majority`) and should be avoided in production whenever possible.

A slightly safer option (Figure 5-7) is to use a five-member set with a write concern of 3 (rather than `majority`) and with two data-bearing nodes in each data center. In this case, when a single data-bearing node fails, the write concern still allows writes. However, should any entire DC fail, we again cannot write safely to our deployment.

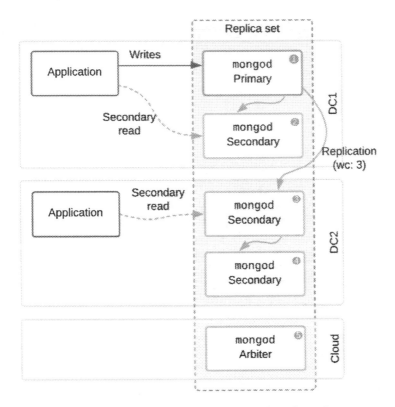

Figure 5-7. *A PSSSA topology, with arbiter in the cloud and write concern: 3*

This topology has another benefit. Because one secondary is in the same DC as the primary, it will have very low latency and should be able to keep up with replication more easily. Should the primary fail suddenly, mongod₂ will normally replicate writes first and be able to take over the primary role faster than any remote member could.

Manual intervention

Let's assume we have a P|S|A topology and that one of the two data centers becomes unavailable due to a massive power failure in that region. The arbiter in the third location has preserved the quorum of voters and so the primary node can remain primary. However, now there is only a single data-bearing node available. Any writes requested with write concern `majority` will be blocked, waiting for a second data-bearing node to acknowledge the change.

Note that an arbiter will always have priority of 0 since it has no data and so can never be primary.

For the purposes of this section, let's consider a default configuration for a PSA replica set.

Listing 5-3. Example replica set configuration with an arbiter

```
{
    "_id" : "rs0",
    "version" : 1,
    "protocolVersion" : NumberLong(1),
    "members" : [
        {
            "_id" : 0,
            "host" : "mongodb0.example.local:27017",
            "arbiterOnly" : false,
            "hidden" : false,
            "priority" : 1,
            "votes" : 1
        },
        {
            "_id" : 1,
            "host" : "mongodb1.example.local:27017",
            "arbiterOnly" : false,
            "hidden" : false,
            "priority" : 1,
            "votes" : 1
        },
        {
            "_id" : 2,
            "host" : "mongodb2.example.local:27017",
            "arbiterOnly" : true,
            "hidden" : false,
            "priority" : 0
            "votes" : 1
        }
    ],
    "settings" : {
        ...
    }
}
```

The majority for writes is normally calculated based on the number of **voting data-bearing** nodes in the set. Normally setting votes: 0 for the secondary in the rs.config is not enough; however, there is a special case for a PSA topology. So, in this case, you would remove the votes for the unavailable secondary node, but keep the node as a member of the set, as follows:

```
conf = rs.conf();
conf. members[1].votes = 0;
rs.reconfig(conf);
```

This would give the votes for the primary node to continue and also allow the application's request for majority write concern to be satisfied by the single data-bearing node. The unavailable secondary will attempt to catch up replication as soon as it comes back online. A secondary offline for any extended period of time in a replica set with many write operations may be unable to catch up on oplog changes and need a full resync.

Don't forget to **restore** voting rights once the unavailable member is back online.

Reading and latency

When components are deployed in multiple physical locations, DC to DC latency can become a major issue for performance. We firstly want to maintain our fault tolerance as much as possible and secondly want to achieve high throughput by having low-latency data flows, but thirdly don't want to waste computing resources by having entire components underutilized while the system is in a healthy state.

Warning   The counterargument to not reserving any resources on effective standby is that when any one component fails, performance will drop.

When building replica sets with many data-bearing secondary nodes, there are some use cases where reading from secondaries becomes a desirable option.

Let's imagine the PSSSA (Primary, 3 Secondaries, and Arbiter) deployment in Figure 5-8 which has two application servers active, one in each data center.

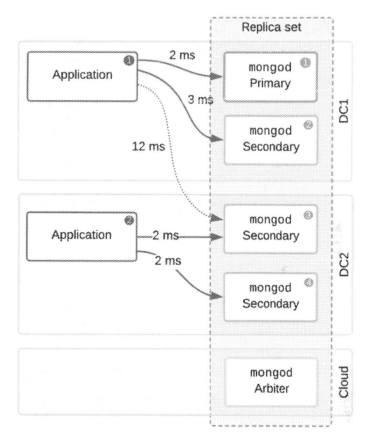

Figure 5-8. *A PS|SS|A replica set with applications in two data centers*

Nearest preference

If the nearest preference is requested in the connection string, Application (1) will read from either mongod (1) or (2) since the RTT is 2 and 3 milliseconds, respectively, and the nodes in DC2 exceed the latency window. Application (2) will tend to read from mongod (3) or (4) **except** if the replication lag exceeds maxStalenessSeconds. In this case the driver will choose to read from mongod (1) or (2). If maxStalenessSeconds is not specified, only the RTT latency will be considered for node selection.

Primary preferred reads

If, on the other hand, primaryPreferred was requested, both Applications (1) and (2) will read from mongod (1) since it is the current primary. However, if the localThresholdMS is set to 5 milliseconds, then the primary in DC1 is considered too far away, and so mongod (3) or (4) will be selected.

Three data center scenarios

A topology with data-bearing MongoDB nodes distributed evenly across at least three data centers is the ideal situation. In Figure 5-9 we can see a topology with optimal redundancy in a PSS topology. Any single data center can be lost, while an application is writing with write concern `majority` to ensure distributed durability and ensure against data loss. Furthermore, if subsequently a second data center also fails, there is still no data loss, but some manual intervention would be required to force the remaining data-bearing node to accept writes.

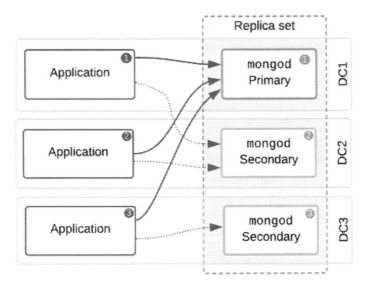

Figure 5-9. *A 3-DC, 3-node topology with optimal redundancy*

Some architects choose topologies with multiple nodes per data center, for example, a PS|SS|S topology (see Figure 5-10). In this case, an entire DC can be lost without affecting availability; however, often this design is chosen to allow secondary reads. In this case, however, a loss of a data center will also result in a *drop of performance* since less nodes will be responding to read requests. For critical applications with strict performance targets or clusters which are underprovisioned for their current workloads, this can have considerable impact.

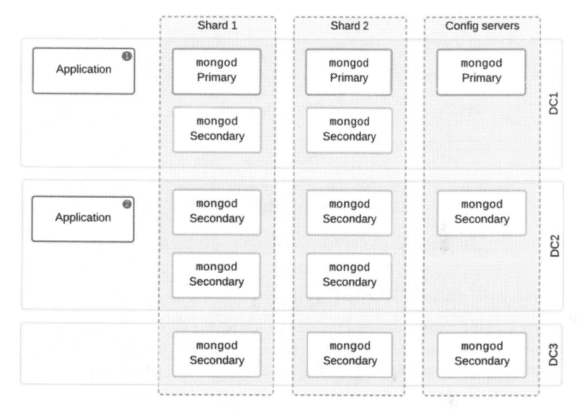

Figure 5-10. *A sharded cluster in 3 DCs with PS|SS|S shards*

A more cost-effective approach is to use one **fewer** node overall and instead create three shards each with three data-bearing members (Figure 5-11). This has the same redundancy profile should a single data center fail, but gives us three shards each with a primary node that can accept writes. Should you choose to do secondary reads, you have only six secondaries overall, but each has less data and can keep a larger proportion in its memory cache, giving much better per-node performance for the same hardware profiles.

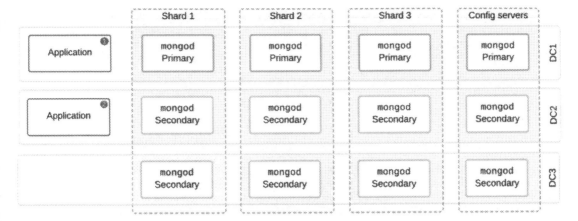

Figure 5-11. *A sharded cluster in three DCs with P|S|S shards*

Load and performance testing

When building a cluster for the first time, and preparing to launch a new application with MongoDB, it's important to always *performance test* to ensure that expected performance can be achieved on a small scale. You should also *load test* to ensure correct behavior of all components, before moving to production-scale data. This section considers a few common situations that can be experienced when testing.

Overloaded connections

It's important that any application is able to respond correctly to slow responses and timed-out connections. If you get to a point where the shards themselves are not able to service incoming operations in a timely manner, then the connections will build up on the mongoses. By default, a mongos will allow up to 64k connections before it starts refusing new connections from an application. Be aware that every 1k connection requires almost 1GB of RAM in overhead. Therefore, if you are running a mongos on a VM with limited resources, you are likely to hit this limit much earlier. Running on most Linux variants, an Out-of-Memory Killer (OOM Killer) will activate and kill the process with the most resident memory usage. In a production system, with many mongoses, the application will then continue routing requests to surviving mongoses which may now be even more loaded than before, causing a cascading effect.

Timeouts

Most MongoDB drivers include an option to set a maxTime or maxTimeMS on query operations. This allows the application to set a server-side time limit on any operation, for example, 3000 for a 3-second limit. This value is passed to the server along with the initial request, and a timer on the server side will automatically terminate an incomplete operation after this time and cleanly release server resources. This can be very useful to avoid using excessive server resources during unexpected load or on an unstable network. If an application drops the connection for some reason, or the connection times out due to a very long query, we can be assured that its impact on server resources will be limited.

On the other hand, setting very low connection timeouts can have the opposite effect. Imagine the client has set a 3-second timeout on the connection but is requesting a complex aggregation pipeline which will take 5 seconds to complete. If the application's connection is auto-closed after 3 seconds, and tries again, the server will spend 2 seconds finishing the first pipeline, and *at the same time,* it will start the same pipeline over again as the client re-requested it. This has two negative effects: extra load on the server and a potential infinite loop as the application keeps trying a heavy operation.

Application back-off logic

The solution to applications causing server overload is to add *back-off logic* into the application. In essence, an application should be able to detect that the server is under load and slow down operations. One approach is to use an increasing pause between attempts. After an initial failure, the application waits 1 second before retrying. If that fails again, it could wait twice as long before trying again. This lets the application auto-try without performing a "denial-of-service" attack on its own database server.

Retryable writes and reads

In MongoDB 3.6, drivers gained the ability to retry writes and reads **once** in case of certain failures (such as a transient network issue or a replica set primary failover). This gives stability improvements from the application perspective, without the risk of overloading the server.

Retryable writes was made the default behavior in drivers designed for MongoDB 4.2 and later and can be controlled with the Connection URI options of `retryWrites` and `retryReads`.

Degraded testing

When you start having multiple data centers or larger clusters, the possibility of network issues increases dramatically. With multiple network switches and Internet backbones, there are many points of failure. Since the TCP layer adds automatic retries of packets and routing around failures, it's often possible that complete routing failures can be avoided, but then performance will be severely affected.

It's important to be able to simulate such degraded networks when building a cluster to properly test failover handling and to ensure that all components in the MongoDB cluster are sufficiently provisioned and configured to deal with such events elegantly.

Network saturation

You may have a situation where some other workload on the network is enough to saturate a certain switch, which causes extreme packet delays for a certain subnet and a few nodes out of a sharded cluster. If the affected nodes are hosting secondaries, even regular periods of degradation may not be evident.

However, let's imagine an election has taken place due to planned maintenance on the current primary's host and one of the affected nodes becomes the new primary. Now a shard primary is affected by this network saturation, and suddenly connections are failing with socket timeouts. How do we diagnose and fix such situations?

Diagnosis

Here, we'll mention a few approaches and tools that can be useful:

`ping <hostname/IP>`

This common tool can be very useful for confirming that a hostname used in a replica set configuration actually resolves to the expected IP address and has a valid route. This can be particularly problematic in mixed on-prem and cloud data centers connected via a virtual private cloud (VPC).

`netstat -s`

This command outputs a summary of key networking metrics from the perspective of this host, including historical information about total number of packets sent and how many packets have been delayed or lost.

If packet loss is observed, the next step is to identify where the packet loss begins to occur. `traceroute` (Linux) or `tracert` (Windows) can be used to check each hop along the path to the destination.

```
tcpdump -i any -w /tmp/out.file
```

This is a common packet analyzer that can also capture all TCP packets being transmitted or received over a network, with optional filtering by port or remote host IP. Once captured, data can be visualized in **Wireshark** to follow the flow and debug issues such as TLS handshakes or unexpectedly dropped connections.

```
iftop
```

Similar to `top` and `iotop`, this tool shows a summary of current network traffic grouped by remote host. This can be very useful to monitor actual peak bandwidth during an initial sync or to monitor replication traffic.

iPerf3

iPerf3 is a cross-platform tool for measuring the maximum achievable bandwidth on IP networks. It can be used to simulate realistic MongoDB traffic with multiple simultaneous connections, running for a set time with periodic reporting output.

For example, the following commands set up a client and server and runs a bidirectional test with 50k TCP packets and 15 parallel streams, measuring bandwidth in both directions.

Server: `iperf3 -s -f K`

Client: `iperf3 -c <server IP> -f K -w 50K -R -P 15 --get-server-output`

Common causes of packet loss

Packet loss on a network can occur for a variety of reasons. If you're experiencing packet loss, the following sections describe some possible problems that you can look for.

Link congestion

This can occur when too much traffic is being pushed through a saturated network (or a single switch) with the result that some packets may be dropped.

If it's not possible to reduce network pressure by introducing more efficient queries, do less shard balancing, or change write patterns to reduce the oplog.

In reality, however, increasing bandwidth is the fastest and most cost-effective approach.

Faulty protocol configuration

Occasionally, a maximum transmission unit (MTU) or duplex mismatch on two network devices in the transfer path can result in collisions and ultimately packet loss on the link.

A duplex mismatch can often be recognized because it causes asymmetric packet loss (i.e., in only one direction) and because the packet loss is consistent. In most cases with modern hardware, enabling duplex autonegotiation will resolve the mismatch.

Incorrect firewall configuration

An incorrectly configured firewall can remain undetected until an election occurs. Imagine a secondary node that is able to replicate from a certain host when the primary is in the same subnet, but when an election causes a different host to become primary, a misconfigured firewall rule causes all incoming packets to be dropped. Since all nodes will continuously attempt to send health check pings, you should already see warnings in the logs.

Note   Any warnings in MongoDB logs should be taken seriously and rectified as soon as possible. While they may not seem to be having any negative effects, it may indicate a source of downtime should the state of the cluster change.

Faulty hardware or software

There are a number of other uncommon cases that can cause sudden drops in network performance, such as overheating switches, faulty cables, and so on. Network switches have their own processors and have been known to contain software bugs which cause packet handling or routing to fail during certain edge cases.

In other cases, malware which has infected machines inside the network can cause sudden spikes in traffic which impacts normal MongoDB traffic much like an internal denial-of-service (DoS) attack.

Troubleshooting tips

This section introduces a few tips when planning a complex deployment to make troubleshooting and maintenance easier as components are added over time.

Ports

When building out even a relatively simple sharded cluster, there are many different types of components that will be running, including config servers, mongos routers, and shard mongod nodes. Even when running each component on its own VM and unique hostname, it is strongly recommended to use a standardized port numbering schema across the organization as shown in Table 5-3. This allows system administrators, DBAs, and any third-party monitoring or support tools to quickly identify the role of each node.

Table 5-3. *An example allocation of ports based on role of components*

Component	Process name	Port
Config server	mongod	27019
Standalone node	mongod	27016
Shard node, or replica set member	mongod	27018
Shard router	mongos	27017

If there is an error message in a log or reported via the driver to the application, we can see quickly if it's related to a config server or a shard node by its port number alone.

Time zones

When using data centers in multiple countries, and to simplify troubleshooting from logs from multiple different components, it is recommended to set all hosts' system clocks to Coordinated Universal Time (UTC).

Note   The abbreviation UTC is a compromise solution since the English proposed CUT (for "coordinated universal time") and the French TUC (for "temps universel coordonné").

Some agents and drivers will always log in UTC, so by forcing this time zone setting deployment-wide, it makes it much easier to align different components timelines in logs to debug any issues.

On Linux systems, forcing UTC/GMT can be set with

```
ln -sf /usr/share/zoneinfo/Etc/UTC /etc/localtime
systemctl restart rsyslog
```

Key takeaways

This chapter has covered a lot of detail about MongoDB deployments on different data center configurations.

The key takeaways are as follows:

- MongoDB components need to be able to communicate with each other to transfer data and share health information.

- A configuration with three data-bearing nodes across three data centers is the recommended topology to maximize availability and redundancy.

- Many MongoDB components (including the drivers and `mongos` routers) automatically consider round-trip time when choosing where to query data.

- It's important to test any configurations for performance before moving into production.

CHAPTER 6

Global Topologies

This chapter continues with a deeper dive on topology recommendations for different types of global sharding options depending on whether low latency or data control/ sovereignty is the priority.

Key concepts

Before exploring some practical details about different global topologies, let's review our understanding of sharding and **zones** in particular.

Chunks, splitting, and migration

As you will remember from Chapter 1, when sharding a collection, documents are broken into chunk ranges based on the shard key, and these chunks are distributed across the available shards. Chunks are normally capped at 64MB to allow reasonably quick migrations when necessary.

After many inserts, these chunks will be split into smaller chunks and may be migrated from one shard with too many chunks to another shard that has fewer. The goal of this subsystem is to equally balance the number of chunks between all available shards.

So even if we start off with one shard having documents with field `country` equal to "US", and another shard having all the documents with value "UK", there's no guarantee by default that this will remain the case forever.

© Nicholas Cottrell 2020
N. Cottrell, *MongoDB Topology Design*, https://doi.org/10.1007/978-1-4842-5817-0_6

Shard key

Chapter 1 introduced the shard key as a collection-specific setting which defines which fields from the documents will determine the chunk range and ultimately to which shard the document will be routed.

When using a **compound** shard key, the combination of fields determines the chunk. When we plan geographic distribution of data on MongoDB, the first field of the shard key **must** be the geographic component (country code, zip code, etc.) to allow for grouping of chunks.

Note   When setting up any type of zone sharding, avoid using hashed shard keys since the zone is based on the hashed value of the entire key and so it's impossible to control where ranges of the original value will be. See Chapter 11 on extreme sharding for more details.

Global sharding

For any large application with a user base outside a single city or state, it becomes important to consider sharding by region. There are numerous reasons for this, including reducing the latency (round-trip from application to primary node), the cost of bandwidth (usually incurred between data centers/regions even on the same cloud provider), and compliance readiness. MongoDB provides the ability to design and build a topology which meets all these needs without sacrificing the high availability and redundancy which is so essential for most production workloads.

Bandwidth requirements

Imagine you are running a US-based business with half of the customers residing on the east coast and the other half in California. A single replica set, while providing high availability, will require that all data is replicated across the set with Californian data stored in Virginia and vice versa. The best solution is to move to a sharded configuration even if the data size is not approaching our 2TB heuristic for shard size.

In Figure 6-1, we see a sharded cluster with one shard in California and one in Virginia. Each data center has its own application server and mongos router. The zone sharding has been configured by state so that customer data is stored approximately on the shard closest to them.

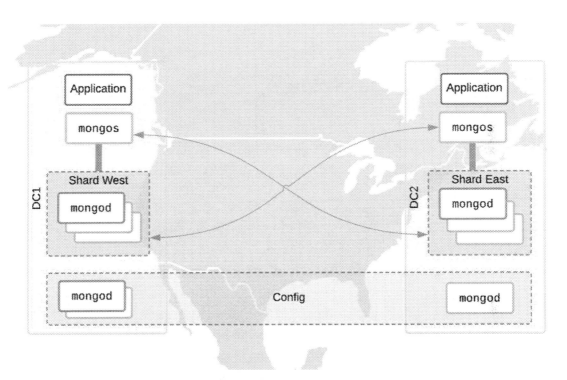

Figure 6-1. *Sharding to minimize bandwidth requirements*

Using similar DNS routing service available in AWS or other providers, customers are also routed to the application server closest to them. In most cases, data will be transferred within the data center, although in some cases some queries may need to be routed to the other data center. Operations on unsharded collections, such as system-wide configuration, may still hit the "remote" shard.

Note that we leverage the multiple data centers to keep a copy of the config replica set in DC2. Remember that the config database contains critical mapping data for which chunk ranges reside on which shard.

There are certain downsides with this approach. One is that all three copies of the West data are in the same region. This risk can be somewhat minimized by hosting each node in a separate availability zone (AZ). Otherwise, region-wide problems could take down an entire shard and any unsharded collections stored there.

Low-latency requirements

The most common reason for global sharding topologies is to minimize latency for the end users. On a global scale, the only way to achieve this is to partition the data based on the likely location of the customer and allow writes and reads via MongoDB nodes in a geographically close data center.

Setting up a zoned cluster

In this section, we'll work through an example of using zoning rules on a global cluster as its needs change over time.

Defining zones

We can imagine zones as a contiguous administrator-defined range of shard key values. A zone could initially contain no or few chunks of documents, but in large production systems, there could be hundreds or even millions of chunks.

In Figure 6-2, we can see two zones defined for the customers in the United States (with country code "US") and customer from the United Kingdom (defined with the ISO 3166-1 standard country code "GB" for Great Britain).

In this example, we are still assuming that the customer ID field custId is actually a unique field across the cluster, but because we have a compound shard key, there is a chunk region starting with a negative infinity value of custId for both "US" and "GB" chunks.

Note   In the following diagrams, -∞ is actually represented internally as the special BSON value MinKey and ∞ by MaxKey.

Shard key: {country: 1. custId: 1}

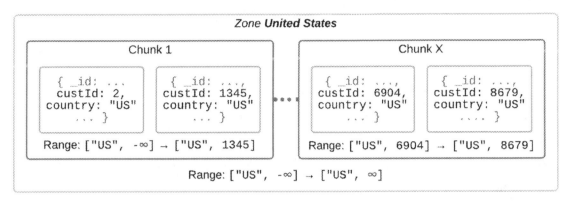

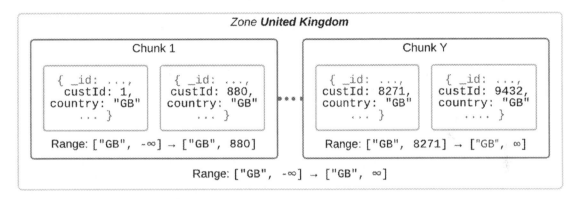

Figure 6-2. *An example of zones and their chunks*

Defining only two zones in our system in this way does not limit us from inserting documents with other values for country such as for Canada "CA" or France "FR". It simply means that we have no specific zone for documents with these values. We are allowing the built-in balancer to define a chunk range and automatically choose a shard to store these documents. This happens completely automatically and instantly.

Note that zone ranges may not overlap, and ranges are always inclusive of the lower boundary and exclusive of the upper boundary. This makes it obvious to all mongos routers as to which shard a new document should be inserted.

Mapping zones to shards

Let's imagine that we have three shards available in our cluster: one in US-East, one in the EU-West, and one in Singapore. We're mostly concerned with our customers in the United States and the United Kingdom at the moment, and we want to make sure that their data is stored inside their respective countries. For all other customers, we are happy to have the data stored anywhere for now.

Note   A single shard can host multiple zones. Furthermore, a zone can be associated with multiple shards.

In Figure 6-3, we see that customers in the United Kingdom and the United States match our zone rules, and those zones are each mapped to one particular shard. The customers from India ("IN") and France ("FR") could be located on any shard. In fact, the chunks for France are likely to be migrated to the Singapore shard since that doesn't have as much data.

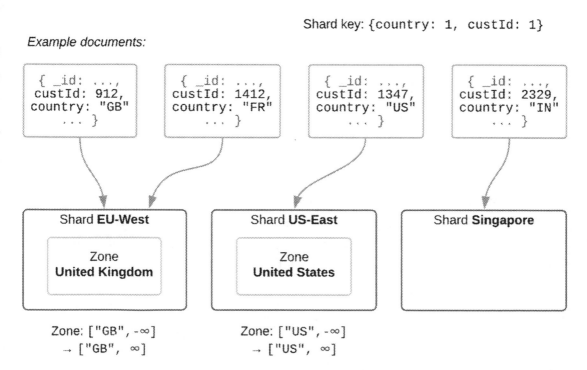

Figure 6-3. *Example documents assigned to zones*

Now let's imagine that we launch in India, and due to some new regulations in that country (see Chapter 4 on data compliance regulations), we need to keep all Indian customers' data inside the country. We can do that by adding a new zone.

Adding new zones

We first need to specify a new zone to constrain documents where `{country: "IN"}` such as with the following command.

Listing 6-1. Define a new zone range named "IND" for India

```
sh.updateZoneKeyRange("myDB.customers",
  { country: "IN", custId: MinKey },
  { country: "IN", custId: MaxKey },
  "IND");
```

The zone itself doesn't affect the migrations yet since we haven't specified a preference to the balancer for which physical shards these zones should be located.

Note   Both *Ops Manager* and the *MongoDB Atlas* managed service provide a user interface to help define your zone definitions and assignments.

Adding new shards

We now have a zone defined for the Indian customer data. Before we can move any data to the Indian zone, we must first create our infrastructure there and integrate it into the existing sharded cluster. The steps for this are roughly:

1. Provision new servers or VMs in multiple data centers inside the target country.

2. Install dependencies, MongoDB binaries, and storage systems according to the production checklists and security best practices.

3. Build a new replica set with an appropriate name, for example, "sh-india-1". This will allow for easier management later as our cluster grows.

> **Note**   It's always safest to use an automated tool like *Ops Manager* (Enterprise only) or Ansible scripts to avoid human error. See Chapter 7 for more details on deployments and Chapter 5 for more details on replica set topologies.

4. Pause the balancer for now, as we don't want it to start immediately moving any chunks to this shard until zones are properly configured. From a `mongos` run `sh.stopBalancer` (`10*60*1000`).

   Here we pause for only 10 minutes because disabling the balancer for longer periods can also prevent other normal operations such as chunk splits.

5. Now we connect this new unassigned shard into our cluster. From a `mongos` run `sh.addShard("sh-india-1/node1.dc0.india.bigcorp.com:27123")`.

6. Add the zones. From a `mongos` run `sh.addShardToZone ("sh-india-1", "IND")`.

7. Unpause the balancer allowing chunk migration to start to the new shard:

   From a `mongos` run `sh.startBalancer()`.

> **Note**   It's not possible to rename a replica set once it is created, since the name chosen acts like a key for members to recognize each other. Therefore, if sets have a specific purpose or location, it's better to give a descriptive name rather than something like `rs0`, `rs1`, and so on.

Gradual balancing

The balancer process has an explicitly low priority in our sharded cluster. We don't want to impact regular workloads by stealing CPU and network resources to quickly balance a shard. Shards can be involved in at most one migration at a time, either donating or receiving chunks. For example, in a six-shard cluster, you could have up to three parallel migrations at a time between pairs of shards.

For large datasets where up to 2TB of data is being moved to a new shard, you may need to allow for as long as a week for the data to become fully balanced.

Growing zones

Let's image that our business has grown strongly in India and our original Indian shard is approaching our 2TB data size threshold. We want to partition it further to avoid problems in backup and restore times.

We still need to keep our Indian data inside India, so the solution is to deploy a *second* Indian shard and balance our data between the two shards. We already have a zone definition "IND" for our Indian documents, so there are less steps in growing out:

1. Provision new servers or VMs in multiple data centers inside the target country; install dependencies, MongoDB binaries, and storage systems according to the production checklists and security best practices.

2. Build another replica set with a consistent name, for example, "sh-india-2" this time.

3. There is no need to pause the balancer, since existing Indian data is already constrained inside the country.

4. Again we connect this new unassigned shard into our cluster

    sh.addShard("sh-india-2/node5.dc1.india.bigcorp. com:27123").

5. Link this new shard to the existing Indian zone:

    sh.addShardToZone("sh-india-2", "IND")

6. Monitor chunk migration to the 2nd India shard with

    sh.status()

Redistributing zones

Let's image that in addition to the country-specific zone definitions for the United Kingdom, the United States, and India, we also defined a pan-Asian zone to cover all other South-East Asian countries.

133

If we didn't create the "catch-all" Asia zone, then Asian customers could have been automatically balanced to physical shards located in the EU or the United States, making potentially unacceptable round-trip latencies.

We can assign multiple ranges to this *Asia* shard as seen in Listing 6-2.

Listing 6-2. Multiple zone ranges can be assigned to a single zone

```
sh.updateZoneKeyRange("myDB. customers ",
  { country: "JP", custId: MinKey },  // Japan
  { country: "JP", custId: MaxKey }, "Asia")
sh.updateZoneKeyRange("myDB. customers ",
  { country: "KO", custId: MinKey }, // Korea
  { country: "KO", custId: MaxKey }, "Asia")
sh.updateZoneKeyRange("myDB. customers ",
  { country: "TH", custId: MinKey }, // Thailand
  { country: "TH", custId: MaxKey }, "Asia")
sh.updateZoneKeyRange("myDB. customers ",
  { country: "PH", custId: MinKey }, // Philippines
  { country: "PH", custId: MaxKey }, "Asia")
```

Let's say that we have cancelled plans to expand into South-East Asia, but we still have our data center in Singapore. But as shown in Figure 6-4, now we also have two shards in India. The latency between the legacy customers in the rest of Asia is acceptable and so we decide to decommission our Singapore shard and move that data to India.

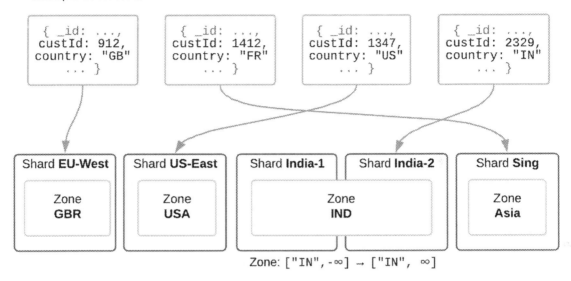

Shard key: {country: 1, custId: 1}

Figure 6-4. *The "Singapore" shard and its Asia zone will be moved to India*

We need to remember that the *Singapore* shard might contain more than just the Asia zone. It may also contain a number of other chunks for customers in countries not specified explicitly in any existing zone.

Draining shards

There are two steps prior to decommissioning the hardware in Singapore:

1. Move the zone to a different shard.

2. Drain the rest of the Singapore shard, thus forcing any "miscellaneous" chunks to be moved elsewhere.

In Figure 6-5, we see the *Asia* zone moved to the *India-2* shard, and by happy coincidence, our nonzoned customer from France was moved to *US-East*.

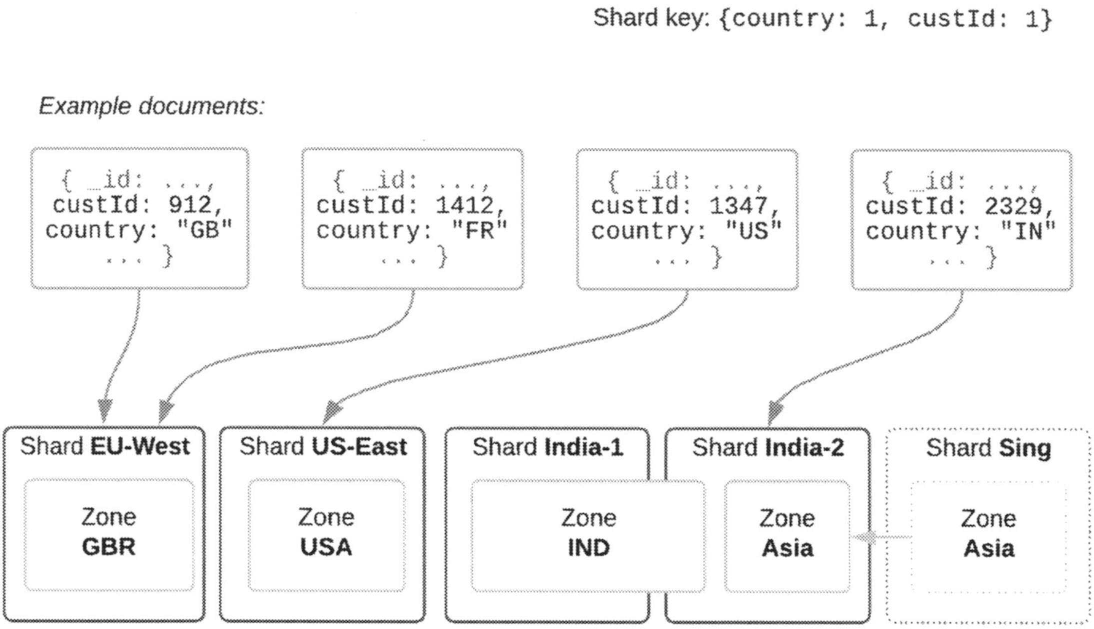

Shard key: {country: 1, custId: 1}

Example documents:

```
{ _id: ...,         { _id: ...,         { _id: ...,         { _id: ...,
custId: 912,        custId: 1412,       custId: 1347,       custId: 2329,
country: "GB"       country: "FR"       country: "US"       country: "IN"
  ... }               ... }               ... }               ... }
```

Shard **EU-West**	Shard **US-East**	Shard **India-1**	Shard **India-2**	Shard **Sing**
Zone **GBR**	Zone **USA**	Zone **IND**	Zone **Asia**	Zone **Asia**

Figure 6-5. *The "Singapore" shard is drained prior to decommissioning*

As our business grows in the United States, we decide to add a second shard in US-West. You may have noticed that we have no way to map customer from California to the West Coast shard and those in New York to the East. Solutions for this requirement are covered in "State-level sharding" later in this chapter.

Check chunk distribution

There are a few simple commands that when run through a mongos, these will give a concise overview of our sharded cluster. The first command is sh.status(), and the following (Listing 6-3) is an example output for our sharded cluster.

Listing 6-3. Example output from the sh.status() command

```
mongos> sh.status()
--- Sharding Status ---
  sharding version: {
      "_id" : 1,
      "minCompatibleVersion" : 5,
      "currentVersion" : 6,
```

```
        "clusterId" : ObjectId("5e41c1b7bb6aba86023a5aa8")
}
shards:
    { "_id" : "sh-eu-west",
        "host" : "sh-eu-west/<host>:<port>,...",
        "tags" : [ "GBR" ] }
    { "_id" : "sh-india-1",
        "host" : "sh-india-1/<host>:<port>,...",
        "tags" : [ "IND" ] }
    { "_id" : "sh-india-2",
        "host" : "sh-india-2/<host>:<port>,...",
        "tags" : [ "IND" ] }
    {  "_id" : "sh-sing",
        "host" : "sh-sing/<host>:<port>,...",
        "tags" : [ "Asia" ] }
    {  "_id" : "sh-us-east",
        "host" : "sh-us-east/<host>:<port>,...",
        "tags" : [ "USA" ] }
active mongoses:
        "4.2.3" : 3
autosplit:
        Currently enabled: yes
balancer:
        Currently enabled:  yes
        Currently running:  no
        Failed balancer rounds in last 5 attempts:  0
        Migration Results for the last 24 hours:
                2 : Success
databases:
        {  "_id" : "config",  "primary" : "config",  "partitioned" : true }
        {  "_id" : "myDB",  "primary" : "sh-eu-west",  "partitioned" :
        true,  "version" : {  "uuid" : UUID("b366477f-afa9-4b95-924e-
        d916cc56d9e8"),  "lastMod" : 1 } }
            myDB.customers
                shard key: { "country" : 1, "custId" : 1 }
```

```
            unique: false
            balancing: true
            chunks:
                sh-eu-west     1
                sh-india-2     1
                sh-us-east     1
                   { "country" : { "$minKey" : 1 },
                     "custId" : { "$minKey" : 1 } } -->>
                     { "country" : "IN",
                      "custId" : { "$minKey" : 1 } }
                       on : sh-us-east Timestamp(4, 0)
                   { "country" : "IN",
                     "custId" : { "$minKey" : 1 } } -->>
                     { "country" : "IN",
                      "custId" : { "$maxKey" : 1 } }
                       on : sh-india-2 Timestamp(3, 0)
                   { "country" : "IN",
                      "custId" : { "$maxKey" : 1 } } -->>
                     { "country" : { "$maxKey" : 1 },
                       "custId" : { "$maxKey" : 1 } }
                        on : sh-eu-west Timestamp(4, 1)
                     tag: IND  {
                        "country" : "IN",
                        "custId" : { "$minKey" : 1 } } -->>
                      { "country" : "IN",
                          "custId" : { "$maxKey" : 1 } }
```

We will go through this `sh.status()` output section by the following section.

Shards

As the name suggests, the **shard** section lists all the configured shards in this cluster. Each shard should list all known nodes in that shard's replica set as a sort of seed list. In reality, this would be something like:

```
sh-india-2/host5.dc1.india.bigcorp.com:27123, host6.dc1.india.bigcorp.
com:27123, host7.dc1.india.bigcorp.com:27123
```

For the same reasons of high availability, we should really include all nodes when configuring the shard in the configuration.

If `host5` happened to be down when this `mongos` started up and fetched this config from the `config` database, it would still be able to connect to the other nodes and from their autodetect other parts of the replica set.

Active mongoses

The **active mongoses** section simply lists the total number of `mongoses` available in the deployment and their binary versions.

Note   The drivers in your application will only connect to the `mongoses` listed out in the Connection URI and will not auto-discover other `mongoses` in the deployment. This can be useful to reserve some `mongoses` for special workloads.

Splitter/balancer

The splitter and balancer are closely related modules in the automation of a sharded cluster. The splitter identifies chunks that are too big and splits them into two smaller chunks.

While the overhead of individual splits is pretty small, the result of splitting up chunks unnecessarily is more complex metadata and the less efficient routing of queries to target shards.

Note that splits will only be triggered during inserts or updates of documents into that particular chunk range. The **autosplit** enabled simply means that these splits can occur, even if there are currently no migrations allowed.

In Figure 6-6, you may notice that a split produces chunks that preserve the bounds of their parent. A split operation never requires migration to another chunk, nor can it invalidate zone rules. By extension, any data protection regulations that require user documents to exist in a certain physical location are not violated.

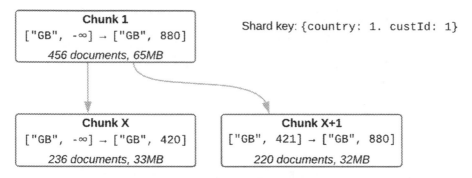

Figure 6-6. *A large chunk is split into two child chunks*

Once the chunk has been split into two, the balancer may be triggered if an imbalance between the shards is detected. In the sh.status() output earlier, we see that the balancer is enabled, but it is currently not running since no shards are out of balance and all chunks already follow the zone configuration. Should we change the zone ranges, the balancer may need to start moving chunks to a new shard to match the zone configuration.

Note   You should avoid disabling the splitter or balancer for long periods as shards may become unbalanced, especially during import workloads.

Databases

This section lists every database known on this cluster.

If the database is listed as partitioned: true, then it is sharded. There may be some smaller databases that are not partitioned at all, and can have no sharded collection.

Notice that our customers database has a primary shard listed. The primary shard is the location of all unsharded collections and can be considered as a "home" shard for that particular database. Any non-sharded collection will exist only on that shard. This makes it easy for the mongos router to target a particular shard for these smaller collections.

Some basic metadata is also displayed here, such as the shard key and whether it has a unique constraint applied. Next, a summary of chunks is listed so that we can quickly see if each shard has roughly the same amount of data. With no zoning, these should be balanced, but in our global cluster, shards linked to zones with more documents will be larger.

Check existing zones

Before we make any more changes, we want to check that our mappings are as we expect them to be. We can connect via any `mongos` router to query configuration from the `config` database.

The `shards` collection lists all the shards and which zones are mapped to them. The `tags` collection lists all the zones, their ranges, and the tag chosen, such as "IND". This is shown in Listings 6-4 and 6-5.

For example, the following can be run from the Mongo shell.

Listing 6-4. List all configured zone ranges

```
use config;
db.tags.find();
```

Listing 6-5. The tags output shows the ranges and tag

```
{ "_id" : { "ns" : "myDB.customers",
    "min" : { "country" : "IN", "custId" : { "$minKey" : 1 } } },
  "ns" : "myDB.customers",
  "min" : { "country" : "IN", "custId" : { "$minKey" : 1 } },
  "max" : { "country" : "IN", "custId" : { "$maxKey" : 1 } },
  "tag" : "IND" }

{ "_id" : { "ns" : "myDB.customers ", "min" : { "country" : "JP", "custId"
: { "$minKey" : 1 } } },
  "ns" : "myDB.customers ",
  "min" : { "country" : "JP", "custId" : { "$minKey" : 1 } },
  "max" : { "country" : "JP", "custId" : { "$maxKey" : 1 } },
  "tag" : "Asia" }
```

Move a zone

In our case, we want to relocate the entire Asia zone, but not change any of its ranges since the country codes have not changed. This remapping of a zone to a shard can be done with the following commands:

```
sh.removeShardFromZone("sh-sing", "Asia")
sh.addShardToZone("sh-india-2", " Asia ")
```

At this point all *Asia* chunks will start being moved to the sh-india-2 shard.

Drain a shard

To drain the chunks from a shard, we first issue the removeShard command on the shard to remove:

```
db.adminCommand( { removeShard: "sh-sing" } )
```

This will start moving any chunks of documents from sharded databases homed on *other* shards, but requires manual intervention to re-home databases that exist only on this shard. The system cannot automatically decide where to move them.

The removeShard command will return a document telling us the state of the activity and if there are any databases blocking the move.

Listing 6-6. The result of removeShard on a database primary

```
{
   "msg" : "draining ongoing",
   "state" : "ongoing",
   "remaining" : {
      "chunks" : NumberLong(45),
      "dbs" : NumberLong(2),
      "jumboChunks" : NumberLong(0)
   },
   "note" : "you need to drop or movePrimary these databases",
   "dbsToMove" : [
      "db2",
      "db3"
```

```
    ],
    "ok" : 1
}
```

In this case, we will need to manually move two databases: db2 and db3. We can choose to move both to our first Indian shard with

```
db.adminCommand( { movePrimary: "db2", to: "sh-india-1" })
db.adminCommand( { movePrimary: "db3", to: "sh-india-1" })
```

The original removeShard command will need to be rerun again until the response of the state value is "completed". At this point, the shard is drained and the hosts can be taken offline safely.

Goal state

Note that in both cases earlier, the configuration "goal state" is updated immediately in the metadata, but the chunks themselves may take hours or days to fully migrate to satisfy the new configuration. Network bandwidth, other workloads, and the balancer window are all factors that may limit the speed at which the target state is reached.

State-level sharding

If your business is focused on one or many geographically large countries like the United States, China, or Australia having data stored in just a single physical location (such as having all data centers in Virginia, US-East), then the latency to the other side of the country may be just too high for your use case.

The solution is to extend this concept of country-level sharding to state level. Luckily, this is a matter of using something more than just a country code.

Post codes

If you know that you would only ever operate inside the United States, then a zip code might be a good candidate, but to also support international expansion, some sort of compound geographic shard key is more flexible.

Let's imagine you have documents like this structure (Listing 6-7).

Listing 6-7. A document structure to support state-level sharding

```
{ _id: ObjectId(....),
  custId: 1234567,
  name: "John Smith",
  street: "20 W 34th St",
  city: "New York",
  postcode: "10118",
  state: "NY",
  country: "US"

  ...

}
```

Note   You should consider storing zip or post codes as a string rather than numbers, since UK postcodes include uppercase letters. For example, "SW1A 1AA" is the code for Buckingham Palace.

In the case of the preceding document, a shard key such as `{ country: 1, postcode: 1, custId: 1}` would allow both simple country- and region-based sharding initially and then later more complex zoning rules to partition data into more specific location. For example,

```
sh.updateZoneKeyRange("myDB.customers",
  { country: "GB", zipcode: "SW00 000", custId: MinKey },
  { country: "GB", zipcode: "SWZZ ZZZ", custId: MaxKey },
  "UK-London")
sh.updateZoneKeyRange("myDB.customers",
  { country: "GB", zipcode: "SE00 000"", custId: MinKey },
  { country: "GB", zipcode: "SEZZ ZZZ"", custId: MaxKey },
  "UK-London")
```

would define some zones to be homed in a shard physically located in or near London. In Figures 6-7 (United Kingdom) and 6-8 (United States), we can see that specifying exact zone rules for every region would be extremely complex.[1]

---

[1]Maproom https://maproom.net/shop/map-of-uk-postcodes/

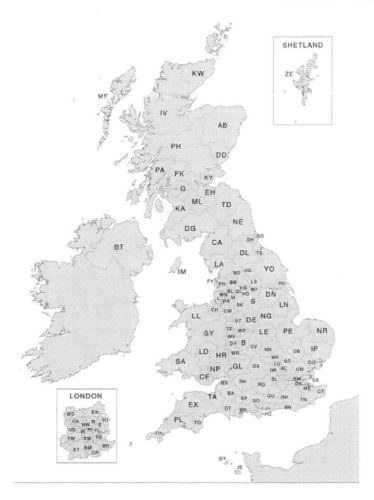

Figure 6-7. *A postcode map of the United Kingdom for subnational sharding*

In the same deployment, rules could be set up to label New York customers and locate them on hardware on the east coast:

```
sh.updateZoneKeyRange("myDB.customers",
  { country: "US", zipcode: "00500", custId: MinKey },
  { country: " US", zipcode: "00600", custId: MaxKey },
  "US-NY")
sh.updateZoneKeyRange("myDB.customers",
  { country: "US", zipcode: "06390", custId: MinKey },
  { country: "US", zipcode: "06390", custId: MaxKey },
  "US-NY")
```

```
sh.updateZoneKeyRange("myDB.customers",
  { country: "US", zipcode: "10000", custId: MinKey },
  { country: "US", zipcode: "14999", custId: MaxKey },
  "US-NY")
```

As you can see in Figure 6-8, the purely numerical approach of US zip codes, and the grouping per state, will make it much easier to define a small set of zone key ranges while still accurately mapping groups.[2]

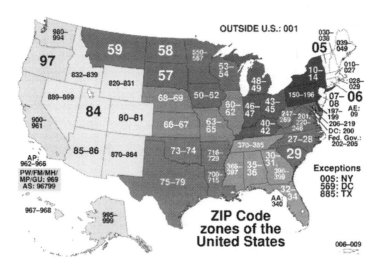

Figure 6-8. *A US zip code map which can be used for zone sharding*

In the United Kingdom, there is no logical geographic connection between the two-letter prefixes, and so a zone key range might need to be defined for every single prefix. You could define ranges for just the high-density areas and allow all others to be homed on a shard in a central DC with reasonably low latency to all parts of the country.

ISO 3166-2

As you can see from earlier, using postcodes for state-level sharding quickly becomes complex. A far superior solution is to use the International Organization for Standardization (ISO) standard 3166-2. This standard provides formal subdivision codes for every country in the world to different levels of specificity.

---

[2]Wikipedia https://en.wikipedia.org/wiki/ZIP_Code#/media/File:ZIP_Code_zones.svg

For the United Kingdom, using the top-level divisions of GB-ENG, GB-NIR, GB-SCT, and GB-WLS for England, Northern Ireland, Scotland, and Wales, respectively, is probably sufficient. Otherwise, 27 second-level county subdivisions are also available, such as GB-OXF for Oxfordshire.

For the United States, there are top-level divisions for all 50 states as well as US-DC for the District of Columbia, as well as codes for other areas like US-GU for Guam and US-PR for Puerto Rico.

In this approach, you would add an additional location field, resulting in documents like:

```
{ _id: ObjectId(....),
  custId: 1234567,
  name: "John Smith",
  street: "20 W 34th St",
  city: "New York",
  postcode: "10118",
  state: "NY",
  country: "US"
  location: "US-NY"
  ...
}
```

Then by using the shard key { location: 1, custId: 1}, you can zone customer data down to whichever subnational division is appropriate.

Reading and scatter-gather

The best way to scale a sharded cluster for reading data is to be able to specify all values for the shard key in every query. That way, the mongos router can request the data from the one shard which contains the data. In our approach so far, we may initially know only the custId value (i.e., from a web or API request), and so every shard in the entire cluster must be queried for a match. Once we have the country and zip code fields also, subsequent queries can filter with all shard key components and target just one shard.

MongoDB Atlas

MongoDB Atlas is a fully managed cloud database. Atlas handles all the complexity of deploying, managing, and healing your global deployments on the cloud service provider of your choice. This service includes a friendly interface to configure and grow your deployment as the business needs become more complex.

This global sharding system uses the ISO 3166-2 country and subdivision codes discussed earlier and requires a field called `location` be combined with another secondary field of your choice.

Figure 6-9 shows the two predefined templates for performant global clusters, one with three zones and another with five zones. These assume at least the same number of shards as zones, so this will require a reasonably large deployment.

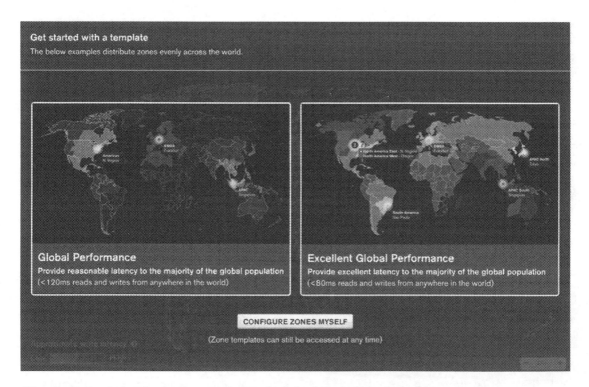

Figure 6-9. *Atlas includes predefined global sharding templates*

In Figure 6-10 we can see a simple interface to define a custom zone based on the number shard locations chosen.

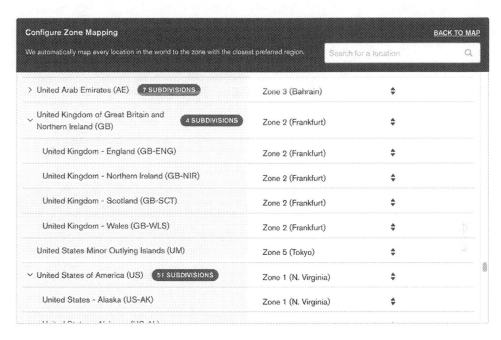

Figure 6-10. *Atlas also includes an interface to map subdivisions*

Summary

In this chapter, we've worked through some examples of a global cluster changing over time. We've also explored some different shard key options for different global sharding use cases. Table 6-1 captures the three shard key patterns covered and their benefits.

Table 6-1. *Summary of global shard options*

Shard key	Pros	Cons
`{ country: 1, custId: 1}`	• Simple zone rules	• No subnational zoning possible
`{ country: 1, postcode: 1, custId: 1}`	• Subnational zoning possible	• Complex metadata and zoning rules
`{ location: 1, custId: 1}` (e.g. Atlas)	• Flexible • Subnational zoning easy	• Requires additional field to be calculated and stored

Key takeaways

From this chapter, the key concepts to remember are as follows:

- Zones can be used to control where ranges of chunks are physically located.

- Each zone can be defined with multiple ranges, so that we could create a single Asian zone with multiple countries.

- A zone can be mapped to multiple shards, so that data in a single zone exceeding our 2TB limit benchmark can still grow within a single region.

- Zones and shards can be added and removed as a deployment grows or the requirements change.

- Zone-based sharding can be used to ensure **low-latency** round-trips between end-user locations and the database or to minimize **bandwidth expenses**.

- Geopolitical sharding rules with zones can also be used to ensure that **data protection regulations** such as GDPR are satisfied.

CHAPTER 7

Deployment and Monitoring

This chapter looks at the most common tools and techniques for automating MongoDB deployments in production, on-prem, and in cloud-based self-managed environments. We also review different monitoring solutions and tips to help DevOps teams avoid issues and react quickly to changes in the deployment.

The DevOps Toolkit

The DevOps toolkit is still evolving very quickly as cloud providers continue to add more features, and large enterprises are moving more of their workloads out into the "public cloud". All details provided are accurate at the time of writing.

Goals

Ideally, our DevOps toolkit should closely mirror our database requirements, namely, *scalability* as the deployment grows, *isolation* of components, *durability* of data, and *performance*.

Community vs. Enterprise

MongoDB Inc. (the company behind MongoDB) chose early to make the database an open source product partly to drive adoption, but also in the belief that an open source database would become more secure, stable, and trusted.

In order to build a business, the company also built some additional features reserved for Enterprise customers. The DevOps tools mentioned in this chapter fall into this category. Any licensed customers are free to use these tools on-prem or on self-

151

© Nicholas Cottrell 2020
N. Cottrell, *MongoDB Topology Design*, https://doi.org/10.1007/978-1-4842-5817-0_7

managed cloud infrastructure and also receive unlimited technical support to ensure their deployments are online and optimal at all times.

MongoDB releases follow the common paradigm of even-numbered releases for production, and odd numbers for preproduction work. For example, version 4.3 is a preproduction release for testing, which is then generally released for production as version 4.4.

Minor releases such as 4.4.1 to 4.4.2 include security and performance improvements, but never break backward compatibility. You should normally upgrade to any minor releases within weeks to benefit from important stability improvements and bug fixes. By contrast, major version upgrades should be tested in a UAT environment with real data and workloads before upgrading in a production deployment.

Ops/Cloud Manager

Ops Manager is the Enterprise management platform for MongoDB which is designed to deploy, monitor, back up, and scale MongoDB deployments on your own infrastructure. *Cloud Manager* is almost identical except that the metrics and backups are stored and managed by MongoDB Inc., but actual user data never leaves your own infrastructure. Table 7-1 shows the differences between Ops and Cloud Manager.

Table 7-1. *A comparison of Ops and Cloud Manager*

	Ops Manager	Cloud Manager
Automates deployments	Yes, on-prem	Yes, on-prem
Monitors deployments	Yes, all metadata and metrics on-prem	Yes, but metadata and metrics in the cloud
Backs up deployments	Yes, backups can be all on-prem (using filesystem, blockstore, or local S3-compatible store), or to Amazon S3 cloud storage	Yes, backups are stored on an Amazon S3 bucket managed by MongoDB the company
Requirements	Automation agents installed on all hosts Replica set to store Ops Manager config (AppDB) Replica set to store oplog and blockstore (for backups) Hosts for Ops Manager instances (plus optional load balancer)	Automation agents installed on all hosts

Both tools are able to help manage, reconfigure, grow, and upgrade versions of your MongoDB deployments all in a *rolling manner* to avoid downtime. For anything more than a single replica set in production, the risk of manually applying updates is otherwise too high.

Rolling changes

When it comes to automating production MongoDB deployments, making rolling changes is critical. Since a well-constructed, healthy cluster will have at least one node of redundancy, it should be possible to upgrade clusters one node at a time, ensuring that all nodes are back online before applying the next changes.

Making multiple changes at once (e.g., restarting two nodes in a three-node replica set) would make a shard become momentarily read-only, blocking an entire application. This sort of rolling logic is a foundational feature of Ops/Cloud Manager and hard to replicate with off-the-shelf DevOps frameworks and custom scripts.

Challenges

As anyone in the DevOps world can attest, *automation is hard*. Automation of complex, distributed systems without downtime is even harder. We want to guarantee that we can perform changes in a repeatable way that is robust and makes it easy to keep components on the latest, most stable, and secure versions. The following are some particular challenges when managing MongoDB deployments.

Changing states

MongoDB *clusters are stateful*. Primary and secondary nodes have particular roles which can change over time. They also have to persist and sync data. We can't just launch a replacement image into a replica set – that would trigger an initial sync – impacting both the sync source and the network. We may need to respect data protection regulations, by tightly controlling the location and flow of data.

Security

We also need to *manage security* in a cluster. This may include creating appropriate x.509 certificates to authenticate cluster membership, retrieving master keys from a KMIP server, or connecting to Kerberos to authenticate new connections. We may need to set up TLS in the right order so that we don't lock ourselves out of the cluster, preventing the completion of changes.

Size and complexity

Managing large MongoDB deployments manually, and configuring each node manually, can introduce a number of risks. These include longer downtime (and possible initial sync due to insufficient oplog), or the introduction of configuration errors. A mature well-tested automated system should remove or at least greatly reduce these risks.

Fault tolerance

Since MongoDB is already *self-healing*, and once a cluster is correctly configured, it shouldn't require much intervention (manual or automated) until such time an upgrade or configuration change is required or hardware needs to be replaced.

System architects can choose the level of fault tolerance suited to their business case. For example, a replica set with five data-bearing members (rather than the usual three) can function with up to two members down.

Framework choice

The technologies and stacks of DevOps move fast. Many of the frameworks and methodologies discussed in this chapter may have changed by the time you read this book. When choosing a framework, there are a few issues to consider.

Reuse

We want to loosely couple our automation components, reusing whatever is already available in the products we use (i.e., Enterprise-only tools like Ops Manager and the Kubernetes Operator), and avoid coding our own configuration/scripts from scratch.

Avoid lock-in

In general, we don't want to overcommit to a particular framework. Even popular solutions may stop receiving support, and we could suddenly find that we can't easily upgrade to the newest, most secure operating system because our tooling just doesn't support it.

We don't want to lock ourselves into our current infrastructure, be that raw metal, OpenStack, OpenShift, hyperconvergence, and so on.

We want to maintain the option to move painlessly to a cloud provider, or even better, to a *multi-cloud configuration* where we don't depend on any one provider. This was particularly painful during the Covid-19 epidemic where those reliant on Azure found that there was simply no capacity available to spin up new *compute instances*.

Multi-cloud topologies

If you plan to deploy to the cloud and maximize high availability, using multiple cloud providers is one option. You could have a European shard with a node in GCP `europe-west3`, Azure Germany West Central, and AWS `eu-central-1`. This would place all nodes in or near Frankfurt, Germany, to reduce latency, but we need to be careful about the costs of bandwidth between providers.

The complexity of multi-cloud DevOps is also higher. Some tools like Terraform include platform-specific modules which can seamlessly deploy the low-level infrastructure. Other tools like Ansible may require custom playbooks for certain cloud providers who offer customized host images, networking stacks, or firewalls.

Base images

Each cloud provider offers a somewhat tailored (and optimized) base image for each Linux flavor. It's tempting to use each provider's image as a foundation, since they come with preconfigured optimizations. To avoid lock-in, you could instead build your own customized images with HashiCorp's *Packer* (`https://packer.io/`) or a similar *infrastructure-as-code* (IaC) tool.

In many cases, it's better to use Terraform to manage any cloud-specific aspects of the environment (e.g., security groups, VPNs, auto-scaling), although there are cloud-specific modules for configuration management tools like Ansible.

Virtual machines

Virtual machines (VM) now form the cornerstone of both on-prem and cloud computing stacks. By breaking up very large hosts into multiple virtual machines, MongoDB deployments can be deployed more efficiently but kept separate. This means that instability in one VM, or one node, should not adversely affect the stability of any others even on the same VM host.

Figure 7-1 shows a single shard cluster spread over eight virtual machines deployed on three physical VM hosts. Any one physical host can fail without affecting the cluster's operation.

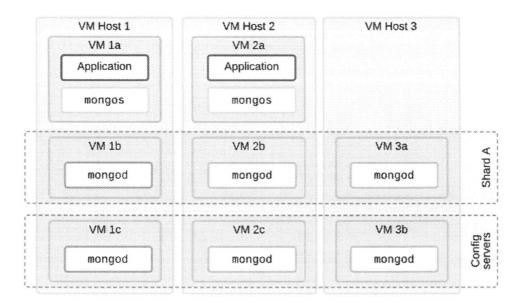

Figure 7-1. *Virtual machines provide resource separation*

Most VM solutions support the concepts of *affinity* and *anti-affinity*. Affinity rules require that a group of VMs should be deployed on the same VM host. By contrast, anti-affinity rules can be used to prevent VMs for a replica set (like 1b, 2b, and 3a) to be deployed on the same host.

Co-location

The issue of "noisy neighbors" stealing CPU and memory resources from other VMs on the same host can still be a problem in the cloud. On-prem, this can normally be configured away by preventing VMs from "borrowing" resources from other VMs.

This lets sysadmins provide consistent resources and guaranteed baseline performance to all processes in a deployment.

Other benefits

VMs also give a number of other benefits, including the ability to more *easily resize VMs* with more computing cores, additional memory resources, and taking *snapshots of storage volumes*.

Containers

Computing containers are another clever way of separating, delivering, and running processes without negatively interacting with others. For MongoDB deployments, a container would include the data files and the config files necessary for a node to start up and reach out to its other cluster members. MongoDB binaries and other required packages can be shared among all the containers on the same host, so they don't necessarily require additional storage space.

Like VMs, containers keep memory, CPU, and I/O resources separate and limited, making it easier to run multiple MongoDB nodes on the same physical host without side effects.

Using `cgroups` in Linux, containers can be configured with resource ceilings, meaning that a config server node can use (for example) only 2GB of RAM, but a shard member on the same host might be allowed up to 200GB.

Compared to VMs

VMs require an entire operating system to achieve the same level of resource allocation, but of course the overhead of running an entire OS inside each VM client wastes a lot of valuable system host RAM.

In Figure 7-2 we see an identical cluster topology to Figure 7-1, except that we have only three VMs. By using containers instead, we can use the host's memory and storage resources more efficiently.

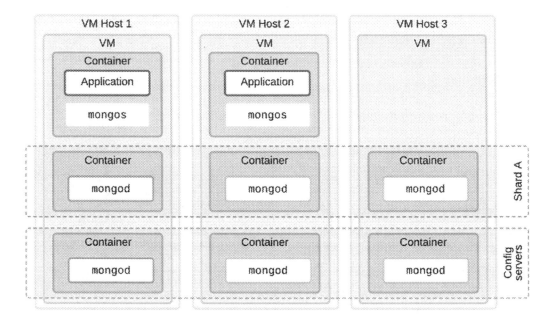

Figure 7-2. *Containers provide separation without VM overhead*

Containers are more lightweight, but often more complex to deploy. They also have tooling better suited to developers, good for organizations using a *continuous delivery* methodology. Using containers also makes testing more accurate since exact containers can be tested and deployed together.

Virtual machines are likely to remain the base level of system administration for at least the near future, as they are the foundation of cloud computing.

Docker

While alternatives do exist (VirtualBox by Oracle, Vagrant, and Wox, among others), *Docker* is currently the most common and easy-to-use container.

Docker provides strong isolation in terms of memory and networking. Ports from these containers need to be explicitly exposed to allow communication to the outside world.

Docker images are often deployed across multiple hosts and data centers using a container orchestration system such as Kubernetes.

Cloud-based container services

Amazon Elastic Container Service (ECS) is a highly scalable container management service for managing Docker containers on a cluster. Amazon Elastic Container Service for Kubernetes (EKS) extends this by adding a standards-based Kubernetes management system for an additional cost.

Other cloud providers offer similar solutions with Azure Container Service (AKS) and Google Kubernetes Engine (GKE).

Hyperconverged infrastructure

Another relatively new technology (as of this book's writing) is *hyperconverged infrastructure* (HCI). One of the goals of this approach is to allow organizations to build up two or more data centers and seamlessly maintain redundant copies of all computing resources. Should a failure occur suddenly in one data center, the system will automatically launch replacement instances of all services in the remaining data centers. This requires that data from one data center is instantly and transparently replicated to the other data centers through a *storage area network* at all times.

Organizations may be tempted to rely on the hyperconvergence framework for maintaining database uptime service-level objectives (SLOs), but mixing MongoDB's highly available replication system and hyperconvergence is both problematic and overly redundant.

MongoDB already includes all the data center and network state awareness but is designed specifically for the control of structured documents. Applications can control their level of redundancy through write and read concerns, giving much more fine-grained control than HCI.

In production, MongoDB can be installed inside hyperconverged infrastructures, but the built-in storage replication should be disabled. MongoDB will handle replication, and the additional load and latency from HCI provides no additional benefit.

Also, if the MongoDB cluster is correctly configured for fault tolerance (Chapter 2) and global topologies (Chapter 6), then losing a single data center should not impact an application. Therefore, booting up a new replacement node immediately after a failure is just not necessary and could add extra load if that node had to initial sync.

Production requirements

The **Production Notes** in your version of the MongoDB documentation is the authoritative reference for how best to configure your server to optimize MongoDB stability and performance.

These notes cover things like what permissions are required on the filesystem, how to set up the journal and logs paths to avoid drive I/O conflicts, network security, WiredTiger cache settings and compression, memory configuration such including NUMA and no transparent HugePages, using XFS and `noatime` for the filesystem, correct network settings (compression, TCP keepalives, etc.), optimizing VM (memory swapping), and how to make SELinux work.

Most of these settings are dependent on the exact operating system and version, the hardware available, and any virtualized environments, so there are no official ready-made virtual images or scripts to prepare the environment. It's up to the system administrator to make sure the servers are set up correctly for the MongoDB nodes that will run there.

Standardized servers

Most organizations choose to run standardized servers for their entire cluster (config servers, `mongos` instances, and shard nodes). If not exactly same specs in terms of memory and storage devices, hosts should have at least the exact same operating system version and security settings.

Any number of automation and orchestration tools can build, prepare, and upgrade servers in a standard, repeatable way to easily replace or add new servers as the database needs to grow over time, or hardware fails and needs to be replaced.

Operating system upgrades should also be made in a prepared, controlled manner and ideally require little or no manual steps to complete.

This way, configuration is at least consistent across the entire cluster, and we can rule out server-level misconfiguration when troubleshooting any changes in behavior or performance of the MongoDB components running on top.

Operation system choices

While MongoDB has been developed to run on a number of popular architectures and OSes in high-performance production-ready configurations, there are just a few which are widely used in production. These include enterprise Linux (Red Hat, CentOS, Oracle, SUSE, Ubuntu Server LTS) and Windows.

Cloud variants

For those running on self-managed cloud hosts, systems like Amazon Linux are also popular since these images already have optimized configurations for the idiosyncratic virtual storage and network implementations. Unfortunately, they are often forks of older versions of Linux, and the location of configuration files and packages included can diverge significantly from standards. This difference makes it even harder to manage a mixed on-prem and cloud environment.

Since you can find official images of most enterprise Linux flavors for cloud providers, it might be best to keep the same OS, but add cloud-specific configuration tasks which configure cloud storage devices different to local hardware RAIDs, for example.

Older RHEL versions

Some older versions of Enterprise Linux can include known security or stability issues. In general, you should plan to upgrade to the latest downstream releases from Red Hat within a year of release.

For example, if you are using native LDAP via the operation system's OpenLDAP library, it's strongly recommended to use at least RHEL 7.5. At this release, OpenLDAP switched to an OpenSSL implementation which brings important thread safety.

MongoDB only provides official packages for Enterprise or LTS (long-term support) releases. Other OS releases do not have sufficiently long support lifecycles.

Virtual machines

If you need to run multiple smaller MongoDB nodes (such as for mongos or config server nodes), it can be tempting to co-locate these on a single server, or VM running on different ports. However, the complexity when troubleshooting such systems and the difficulty ensuring that both processes share system resources in an optimal way is much harder.

It's far better to first set up a VM host and deploy multiple VMs with fixed resources (i.e., with memory ballooning disabled).

Kubernetes

However, for some organizations, VMs are already too cumbersome to manage. Many enterprises have moved their production applications to Kubernetes-based infrastructures like Amazon EKS and OpenShift.

Historically, with the Kubernetes ecosystem it wasn't possible to deploy pods with persistent storage which could survive certain pod moves or hardware failures, making it unsuitable for database deployments. With the addition of `PersistentVolumes` and `StatefulSets`, pods can now be moved without losing data and needing to perform a complete initial sync.

Operators

Kubernetes Operators can be used to package, deploy, and manage MongoDB as a Kubernetes-native application, essentially functioning as a custom controller.

MongoDB Enterprise licenses include access to a Kubernetes operator which together with Ops/Cloud Manager can deploy appropriate *Kubernetes Resource Containers* and then *MongoDB Database Resources* on top. In essence, you can properly automate MongoDB replica sets and sharded clusters inside Kubernetes environments.

Tip   When running applications or microservices inside pods, always set the appName in the connection string. This application name will appear in the log files, and since the IP addresses can change as pods are redistributed, this unique name can help tracking logged issues back to the generating application.

Tools

Infrastructure as code (IaC) is the process of managing and provisioning hosts through machine-readable definition files or scripts that can be easily version controlled and tested. It is a way of encapsulating error-prone manual configuration procedures like run books into software code that makes actual deployment streamlined, reliable, and infinitely scalable. The most common IaC tool today is Terraform.

Continuous configuration automation (CCA) tools can be thought of as an extension of IaC frameworks, but also the *provisioning* and configuration of applications and services on top of the managed hosts.

Configuration management

We'll quickly review some of the most popular configuration management and automation tools: *Ansible*, *Puppet*, and *Chef*. All three tools are open source, very widely used, well documented with great community contributions, but also offer optional paid Enterprise support. They can also work with tools like Terraform to provision the host infrastructure prior to configuration.

Other notable alternatives are SaltStack and Pulumi.

Ansible

Ansible (first released in 2012, and acquired by Red Hat, Inc. in 2015) is an automation platform that allows you to deploy your MongoDB installation and configuration in a simple, repeatable manner. Its paradigm is about configuring simple rules, grouped in fixed-order steps and templates, rather than coding scripts in a procedural language.

It uses SSH to connect from a workstation to multiple remote machines without requiring any special agents on the remote hosts, just its own SSH keys.

Ansible is simple to get started, with a wide user base and lots of examples online. It is also easy to keep changes in source control. However, it's hard to test changes and may require many runs to debug complex tasks grouped into *playbooks*.

Puppet

Puppet (first released in 2005) is model-driven, statically checked, and was built with systems administrators in mind. It follows a client-server (or agent-master) architecture. A commercial version, Puppet Enterprise, is available through Puppet Labs.

The Puppet master compares the current state of the target machine against the machine-level configuration details and then sends instructions to the conversion layer for action. An agent checks regularly for changes and triggers updates.

A module called `puppet/mongodb`[1] (maintained by Puppet Labs and the open source community) manages server installation and configuration of the MongoDB processes, as well as Ops Manager setup. This module has an advanced and complete feature set, including a `mongodb_shard` provider which allows definition of shards and their members. At the time of writing, it supports RHEL/CentOS 5/6/7 and Ubuntu 10 and 12, as well as Debian 6 and 7.

Puppet is a bit more complex than some other management tools (such as Chef and Ansible), but it has a lot of modules that can be used to resolve issues around database management.

Chef

Like Puppet, Chef (first released in 2009) compares host resources against a desired state before making changes on a Chef node. Unlike Ansible, it requires a *Chef client* to be installed on each remote host in order for that host to become a *Chef node*.

Configuration is written into Chef *recipes* which are grouped together as *cookbooks* for easier management. An open source cookbook, *SC-MongoDB Cookbook*[2], is the most advanced preexisting cookbook for Chef and is currently under active development.

On-prem comparison

Any of the three tools presented can be used to prepare dependencies and deploy complex MongoDB deployments. Table 7-2 compares some of the key differences which may help choosing between them based on your platform and infrastructure preferences.

---

[1]https://forge.puppet.com/puppet/mongodb

[2]https://supermarket.chef.io/cookbooks/sc-mongodb

Table 7-2. *A comparison of configuration management tools*

	Ansible	**Puppet**	**Chef**
Architecture	Pushes config (from single node)	Pull (Master-slave)	Pull (Master-slave)
Configuration paradigm	Declarative (Plays and Playbooks)	Procedural (Tasks and Plans)	Procedural (Recipes and Cookbooks)
Update paradigm	Step-based	Idempotent and state-based	Idempotent and state-based
Remote requirements	SSH daemon only, no agent	Master server + Puppet agent	Master server + Chef agent required
Security	SSH key + user privileges	Certificate	SSL and shared secrets
Getting started	Easy	Harder	Harder
Complex tasks	Hard to debug	Powerful	Possible
Platform	Python/pip	Ruby/gem	Ruby/gem
Supported OSes (remote)	Master: Linux/BSD with Python Remote: any POSIX with Python, and Windows	Master: Enterprise Linux, Ubuntu, SUSE Remote: Linux, macOS, Windows, Solaris, and many others	Workstation: RHEL, Ubuntu, Windows, macOS Server: Enterprise Linux, Ubuntu Node/remote: AIX, Linux, BSD, Windows, macOS
Best suited	Initial setup on top of prebuilt VM images or Docker	Regularly changing environments. Where compliance is important.	Regularly changing environments

Automation

Often the goal of CM tools is to standardize and avoid human errors when deploying new hosts and software stacks. With some additional effort, this configuration code can be extended to tear down, move, and scale systems over thousands of nodes, running on different underlying hardware/cloud and on different operating systems.

With awareness of entire systems and dependencies between components, automation can be made to orchestrate changes in a consistent way, for example, to ensure that multiple nodes from the same replica set aren't taken down at the same time.

Provisioning and orchestration

Before we can configure our MongoDB environments and deployments, we may first want to automate provisioning of the hosts. In some cases, we may also need to provision networking infrastructure, storage, and even load balancers.

For most deployments, Terraform is currently the winner in the *infrastructure-as-code* space both for provisioning reproducible on-prem as well as cloud-agnostic infrastructure.

Terraform

While Terraform can also perform configuration, it is currently better to use targeted configuration management tools like Ansible, Puppet, or Chef. Like most CM tools, all Terraform configuration files can be easily version controlled. Custom *Provider* plug-ins can be created in the *Go* programming language.

While possible to use in a free Community version, the maintainer HashiCorp sells an Enterprise version with support.

Purpose

Terraform monitors the state of the environment, and if anything is out of order or missing, it can automatically provide a replacement resource. This is fantastic for environments that require a very steady state.

Cloud infrastructure

Terraform can communicate via cloud provider APIs using standard API keys, in much the same way as on-prem master servers.

Official provider for Atlas

MongoDB Inc. in conjunction with HashiCorp has created an *official provider* that is designed for MongoDB's Atlas fully hosted solution. Currently, there is no official plug-in for using Terraform with non-Atlas on-prem MongoDB deployments.

While it's possible to create a custom or community provider yourself, this can be a very complex undertaking, to build and test a provider. As such, using Terraform **alone** for on-prem MongoDB deployments is not an ideal approach at this time.

Integration with Ansible

Terraform can call Ansible configuration (via Packer) to automate the building up of machine images with MongoDB and dependency packages, and configuration files at the OS level. Terraform can add special tags to your servers for Ansible to find and configure each one accordingly.

In the other direction, Ansible can also be hooked in to the workflow, calling Terraform to launch multiple computing instances based on images already built by Ansible. Often some final steps will be required post-provisioning to actually deploy cluster-specific MongoDB configuration and launch the instances.

CloudFormation

CloudFormation is one of the most popular ways to script the deployment of complex services on Amazon's AWS cloud environment. It allows for both a declarative or programmatic approach to model and provision application environments on the cloud in a repeatable manner.

For example, you could define a CloudFormation script to deploy four EC2 computing hosts, one for the application and three for a MongoDB replica set. This script could ensure that all dependencies and MongoDB libraries are installed via yum, create a config and keyfile for the MongoDB nodes, and ensure that a replica set is initialized once all three nodes are online based on the hostnames allocated.

Unlike the other tools listed here, it is completely closed sourced and has no option for on-prem management.

Kubernetes operator

For Enterprise customers on any sort of self-managed infrastructure, MongoDB offers a custom-built operator using Kubernetes APIs to automate and manage MongoDB clusters.

MongoDB Enterprise Operator for Kubernetes gives you full control over your MongoDB deployment from a single Kubernetes control plane. You can use the operator with any Kubernetes-compatible service such as OpenShift and Pivotal Container Service (PKS).

Kubernetes for MongoDB Atlas

For situations where you are using Kubernetes to deploy applications in fully managed platform-as-a-service (PaaS) contexts, the MongoDB Atlas Open Service Broker can automate your databases on MongoDB's Atlas service on whichever cloud provider is best for your application.

Monitoring

Continuous and automatic monitoring of the health of the deployment, including the detection of anomalies and alerting, is critical to avoid multiple failures and application impact.

Evaluating failure

Depending on the topology and design choices in a MongoDB cluster, there will be different levels of failure which require different urgency to repair. If your cluster has been well designed, any single component failing should not cause application downtime, but you should always react as soon as possible to restore failed components.

Performance

Monitoring the performance and latency of a cluster is one aspect that tends to get less attention until something goes wrong. By understanding the *baseline performance* of your cluster, and its weekly and hourly trends, you should be able to detect abnormal behaviors before they manifest as instabilities or performance drops in your application.

Naturally over time, the size of the database will grow as new users and services are added. Monitoring baselines metrics over time allows *capacity planning*. If you can predict when the current computing resources will be insufficient, you can scale them vertically or horizontally before performance is impacted.

FTDC

One way to understand performance is by analyzing the *full-time diagnostic data capture* (FTDC) metrics generated by each mongod and mongos process and stored in a directory called `diagnostic.data` within MongoDB's `storage.dbPath`.

The FTDC data includes metrics about server, replication, and collection status, as well as connection metrics. It also captures valuable host metrics like CPU and memory usage, I/O, and network usage. These metrics are designed to provide a sort of "black box flight recorder" for telemetry on a deployment to investigate when an issue has been observed.

There will be hundreds of metrics recorded every second, but the format is so compact that a week of metrics require only a few hundred megabytes of storage. There are numerous tools to extract and read this data, including an official open source parsing library written in Go (`https://github.com/mongodb/ftdc`) and an analysis tool called Keyhole (`https://github.com/simagix/keyhole`).

Connection capacity

One example of important metrics captured in FTDC (via the `serverStatus` command) concerns the number of active vs. currently open (but not necessarily active) connections. As each connection takes memory, it's important to set limits to avoid incoming connection storms particularly from microservices or IoT devices (see Chapter 8).

SNMP

Enterprise MongoDB also supports collecting database metrics directly from each node via SNMP on both Linux and Windows into other monitoring solutions. Ops Manager also supports SNMP traps to deliver alerts configured via its Alerts interface.

Alerting

Ideally, someone should be alerted whenever a component fails. To avoid false positives, we may want to wait a few minutes before triggering these alerts to skip short-lived network failures.

It also recommended to temporarily disable alerts during planned maintenance windows when we expect to be shutting down and restarting nodes such as for server maintenance or MongoDB version upgrades.

There are a number of popular generic alerting tools; some which can be configured to check the "liveness" of a MongoDB node by connecting to it on its port, but are unlikely to be able to detect the internal health of the node.

Some monitoring solutions can watch the CPU and memory usage of a process and trigger alerts when these exceed certain thresholds. However, these external views of a process may simply be observing spikes in workload due to legitimately high application traffic.

Prometheus

Prometheus is an open source, community-driven project, which collects, alerts, and stores metrics in a system-agnostic way, and uses its own internal database for storage. It utilizes Grafana (an open source dashboard) to display metrics in various time series views.

Since Prometheus is designed as a generic monitoring solution, there is no built-in mechanism for monitoring MongoDB, but such functionality is supported via plug-ins called *exporters*.

One such exporter is the open source `mongodb_exporter`, currently maintained at `github.com/percona/mongodb_exporter` which responds with metrics to Prometheus server calls.

Enterprise tools

In contrast, the official Enterprise monitoring solutions Ops Manager and Cloud Manager have been built by MongoDB Inc. itself to monitor large clusters, record metrics, and trigger alerts. They are not only able to connect to each node but also *evaluate internal health* to confirm that the node is still able to respond to requests.

Ops/Cloud Manager also records metrics about the load on the node for later analysis and visualization. These metrics are available via a comprehensive API for integration with other monitoring services like New Relic.

Alerts configured in Ops/Cloud Manager can be sent through your existing Alerting tools, via integrations with PagerDuty, Flowdock, HipChat, Opsgenie, Datadog, Slack, and others.

Key takeaways

From this chapter, the key concepts to remember are as follows:

- Provisioning, orchestration, and configuration tools are complex and evolving quickly, with no single standard for deploying MongoDB cluster infrastructure.

- Since MongoDB is stateful and self-healing, the usual tools for auto-scaling application servers can't be easily repurposed.

- Terraform is a popular tool for on-prem and multi-cloud provisioning, with Ansible a good choice for configuration management.

- For Kubernetes infrastructures like OpenShift, an official Enterprise-only operator plug-in is available to provision and configure MongoDB clusters.

- It's critical to properly monitor a cluster to understand baseline performance, both for setting alerts at the correct threshold and also to know when it's time to scale the cluster.

- Enterprise tools like Ops/Cloud Manager are the best choice to automate and monitor large, complex clusters as well as to integrate with existing monitoring/alerting systems like Prometheus or New Relic or via SNMP.

- For best security and stability, you should not wait to upgrade to the latest minor release of MongoDB and OS minor releases.

CHAPTER 8

Special Use Cases and Configurations

Apparently, there is redundancy in memory: You store the same memory in different parts of your brain for accessing at different speeds. That speed would depend on the frequency of use and the importance of the knowledge.

—Bill Nye, mechanical engineer and "Science Guy"

In this chapter, we cover a series of use cases for specific configurations of MongoDB in production, such as hybrid on-prem/cloud clusters, low-latency applications, using an LDAP pool for authentication, and how to store large binary files.

Scaling with secondary reads

In most cases, applications should read and write from the primary node with read preference `primaryPreferred`. Secondaries are intended for high availability and should normally be dedicated to keeping the oplog replicated with the smallest possible lag. They should be ready at any moment to take over from the primary to avoid any application impact that end users could notice.

© Nicholas Cottrell 2020
N. Cottrell, *MongoDB Topology Design*, https://doi.org/10.1007/978-1-4842-5817-0_8

Read preference

However, in certain special cases, where read load is very high compared to writes, and reading slightly out-of-date documents isn't a problem, using the `secondaryPreferred` read preference can be a valid approach. The read preference `secondary` could be used also, but in the rare occasion that a replica set has just a primary node available (perhaps due to an emergency `rs.reconfig()` to remove corrupted/failed hosts), then the application would see no candidate members to read from and stall.

A third option is to use the `nearest` read preference. This will read from secondaries or the primary, but choose among those with the lowest network latency. This could be useful if there are many application servers spread out over many data centers, which are relatively far apart.

In Figure 8-1, we see applications using `nearest` read preference distributed in three data centers, of which DC3 is more remote and suffers from an unstable network connection. This makes the secondary in DC3 lag behind replication by more than 90 seconds.

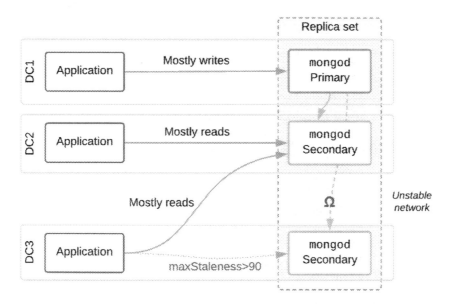

Figure 8-1. *Applications read from nearest node within staleness limit*

Limit staleness

In certain extreme cases, such as when secondary hosts are drastically underprovisioned for the workload, secondaries can fall far behind in their replication. Imagine that you are performing secondary reads, and during peak workloads, the replication is lagging by several hours.

This can be avoided to some extent by specifying a maxStalenessSeconds of 90 in the connection URI string. When set, the driver will exclude from its list of candidates any secondary whose replication is more than 90 seconds behind the primary.

In Figure 8-1 we also see that the application in DC3 correctly ignores the secondary in the local data center due to this excessive replication lag and instead reads from the next nearest node in DC2.

Remember that to avoid *stale* reads completely and therefore to *maximize consistency*, use primary read preference and majority read concern.

Tag sets

Both the read preferences nearest and secondaryPreferred can be combined with maxStalenessSeconds and *tag sets* to control which node is targeted for queries. Let's imagine you have a particular microservice$_A$ which reads only from collectionA and another microservice$_B$ that reads only from collectionB. We could configure tags for the members in the replica set configuration, specify secondaryPreferred read preference, and use different tag set values for each microservice (Figure 8-2). When all nodes are online, drivers would then route traffic for microservice$_A$ (running in DC1) to go to mongod$_1$ and microservice$_B$ (in both DC2 and DC3) to mongod$_3$. This would mean that mongod$_1$ has a working set of mostly collectionA documents in its cache and mongod$_3$ caches mostly collectionB documents. This should result in much less cache churn (and I/O reads) than directing reads at random between the two secondaries.

Since all applications specify tag sets, this setup also means that mongod$_2$ won't receive secondary read traffic at all. In this example, mongod$_1$ happens to be primary, but since no other nodes have a matching {use: "msA"} tag, a read preference of secondaryPreferred by microservice$_A$ will be superseded by the tag match and a primary read will be made instead.

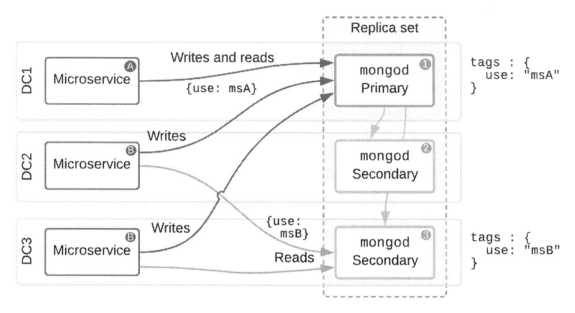

Figure 8-2. *Using different tags to target specific members per application*

Replication behavior will always mean that documents modified via the primary will be loaded into memory on the secondary and may flush out other cached documents.

More background details about read preferences, staleness, and tags are covered in Chapter 5. For exact behavior and syntax, refer to the MongoDB documentation online.[1]

Advanced LDAP with pools

The Lightweight Directory Access Protocol (LDAP) is one of the external authentication sources (along with Kerberos) supported by MongoDB Enterprise. Using LDAP allows you to manage passwords via an existing system such as Windows Active Directory.

Connection management

A simple environment with LDAP providing authentication for your MongoDB deployment might only have a single LDAP server available. In such a setup (Figure 8-3), a failure to connect to the LDAP server for any reason (overloaded server, failed TLS connection, etc.) should ideally be able to retry the LDAP request. In MongoDB 4.0 and earlier, the OpenLDAP/`libldap` library is solely responsible for selecting the LDAP server, establishing the connection, and error handling.

---

[1]`https://docs.mongodb.com/manual/core/read-preference/`

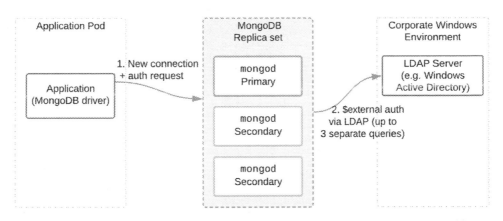

Figure 8-3. *External auth with a single LDAP server*

From MongoDB 4.2, a number of LDAP enhancements such as connection pooling were added, and these greatly improve the performance of LDAP authentication. Originally each connection to an LDAP server was opened up as needed and then closed immediately. As discussed earlier, opening a new connection can add lag to the process. This improvement reuses the pooling algorithms that MongoDB drivers use to keep a pool of connections open to service incoming client requests with lower latency.

Multiple LDAP servers

MongoDB also supports specifying multiple LDAP servers. This can be critical for production deployments that can't afford any downtime due to a failed LDAP request. When the LDAP pool is small and the available LDAP server hostnames don't change, the configuration would be as

```
security:
  ldap:
    servers: ldap1.mycompany.internal:389, \
      ldap2.mycompany.internal:389, \
      ldap3.mycompany.internal:389
```

In Figure 8-4, we see a configuration with three Active Directory servers in a round-robin.

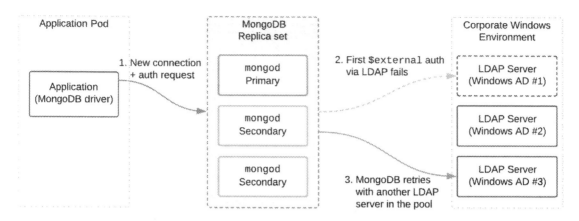

Figure 8-4. *External auth with a pool of LDAP servers*

In this case, the first authentication attempt connected to LDAP Server #1, but this connection failed due to a transient network failure. The OpenLDAP library used by the LDAP authz module will time out after 10 seconds and automatically retry another server from its list. This time, it has connected to Server #3 and has successfully authenticated the user. The initial error will be logged in the mongodb.log, but the only impact to the application is that the connection took 10 seconds longer to connect than usual.

As the authentication process only happens when a new client connection is opened, and if the application has been correctly configured with a connection pool, then new connections will not be established regularly. So the risk of such "stalls" will be infrequent even with unstable LDAP servers.

This approach requires listing the hostnames or IP addresses of all LDAP servers in the pool. For some large organizations, the LDAP servers are managed by a separate team and are subject to change without notice. Therefore, it's not possible to know in advance the hostnames of all the LDAP servers.

One solution is to create a CNAME alias such as ldap-pool.mycompany.internal in the internal DNS which is configured to return the hostnames of all active LDAP servers. However, if you configure your MongoDB nodes with just one entry in servers such as

```
security:
  ldap:
    servers: ldap-pool.mycompany.internal:389
```

then MongoDB and its OpenLDAP library are not aware of the fact that a pool of LDAP servers is available. If the first authentication request to an LDAP server fails, it assumes that the LDAP server is down and will not even attempt a retry. The fix for such situations (at the time of writing) is to specify the same alias multiple times, to force LDAP request retries, that is:

```
security:
  ldap:
    servers: ldap-pool.mycompany.internal:389, \
      ldap-pool.mycompany.internal:389, \
      ldap-pool.mycompany.internal:389
```

Now any transient errors in a single LDAP server will seamlessly retry without surfacing any error to the application at all.

As always, you should monitor MongoDB logs for any errors and react accordingly to correct infrastructure failures before errors start affecting production applications.

Load balancer

The OpenLDAP library itself doesn't maintain any state about the health of the LDAP servers in the pool. If one server is down or unhealthy, authentication attempts may still be routed to this server. MongoDB 4.2 and later have basic health checking which tries to avoid unhealthy LDAP servers. A better approach is to use a dedicated TCP load balancer which is capable of executing LDAP queries as a health check. As shown in Figure 8-5, the MongoDB nodes communicate with the load balancer, which distributes queries to healthy LDAP servers.

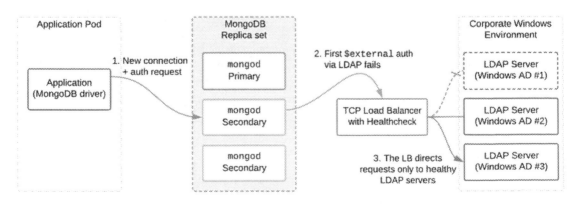

Figure 8-5. *A load balancer proxies and distributes LDAP requests*

This load balancer will normally distribute requests randomly among the backing LDAP servers. Most advanced load balancers will also be able to perform a test LDAP query and check the result. Should any of the LDAP servers not respond in a timely manner, they will temporarily be removed from the pool. This way, any malfunctioning or overloaded LDAP server will be ignored and should not cause MongoDB LDAP requests to stall.

Let's say that the load balancer has a single hostname `ldap-lb.mycompany.internal`. As before, we should list the load balancer's hostname several times in `security.ldap.servers` to ensure TCP-level retries.

Connection timeouts

Choosing the correct timeout values for any sort of distributed system can be tricky. This has also been true for MongoDB in the past, and in early versions some of the default timeout values were not always optimal for large or complex clusters.

The recommendation for any version of MongoDB since version 3.4 is to **use default timeout values for both server and driver configuration** unless absolutely necessary. The default timeouts have been chosen to be optimal for sharded clusters with multiple `mongos` routers and multiple application servers.

Warning   Due to previous default settings, there are a lot of invalid recommendations still online. Many developers and database administrators are tempted to experiment with different combinations of values to try and squeeze out some extra performance, or improve stability during periods of very heavy load.

One risk with a low timeout value is that it will cause connections for operations that are almost complete to be prematurely cut off, leaving the server-side operations to still complete fully. If an operation is then retried, the server will now be running two identical impactful operations in parallel. If allowed to continue, the application runs the risk of launching a type of *denial-of-service attack* on its own database infrastructure.

Limit operation time

To ensure that slow (often erroneous or unexpectedly impactful) operations are killed and free up server-side resources correctly, use maxTimeMS rather than a connection timeout.

maxTimeMS specifies a cumulative time limit (in milliseconds) for processing operations on a cursor. MongoDB does not count network latency between a client and server in this time limit. In-progress operations that exceed the maxTimeMS will be terminated at the next interrupt point when the operation can safely abort.

Timeout details

The *connection timeout* is related to the driver starting/opening a socket connection to the MongoDB node. This is the first step in opening a connection and happens *before* the driver attempts to authenticate. As long as a MongoDB node picks up the incoming connection, this timeout should not be triggered.

The *socket timeout* is about monitoring the continuous incoming data flow. If the data flow is interrupted for the specified timeout, the connection is regarded as stalled/broken. Setting this to a low value (such as 5 seconds) means that if no data is sent/requested for that time, then the connection times out and is recycled. This can create unnecessary connection churn between the application and the MongoDB nodes, which is why no socket timeout is recommended.

The *max wait* is about how long a driver thread will block to get a connection from the connection pool when all existing connections are already in use.

The wtimeoutMS is about how long to wait for a write concern to be handled and can be set differently for each write operation depending on required durability. This is tied to the replication subsystem and is not related to establishing connections between application and MongoDB nodes.

Table 8-1 summarizes the default values for the different waits and timeouts.

Table 8-1. *Timeout descriptions and values from the Java driver*

Setting	Description	Default value
Connection timeout	A value of 0 means never timeout. It is used solely when establishing a new connection `Socket.connect(java.net.SocketAddress, int)`.	10000 (10s)
Socket timeout	It is used for I/O socket read and write operations `Socket.setSoTimeout(int)`.	0 (no timeout)
Max wait	The maximum wait time in milliseconds that a thread may wait for a connection to become available.	1200000 (120s)
`wtimeoutMS`	Corresponds to the write concern `wtimeout`. `wtimeoutMS` specifies a time limit, in milliseconds, for the write concern.	No default
`maxTimeMS`	This is a cursor timeout and not related to the high-level connection timeouts mentioned earlier.	No default

Hybrid cloud models

Imagine you have a sharded cluster with multiple databases running on-prem in two data centers. Your organization has decided that it's time to test running some instances on a public cloud like AWS. Some of the data is more sensitive than others, and it has been decided that a small subset of data, all contained in one collection, cannot be stored on the cloud. One extreme option could be to extract out this data and store it in a separate replica set on-prem.

We are going to walk through an example moving a portion of data to the cloud, but leaving a specific subset of sensitive data in our private data centers.

Managing sensitive data

Extracting data into a completely new and separate deployment would require significant refactoring of existing API calls and application logic. An alternative approach could be to use the concept of a *primary shard* for non-sharded databases to achieve a hybrid approach. See Chapters 10 and 11 for advanced details about sharding.

Note   Any sensitive sharded collections will already be distributed across *all* shards in the cluster. For the following example, it would first require mongodumping and then `mongorestoreing` these collections' data into new unsharded collections.

Considerations

One of the major motivations for moving to cloud infrastructure is the ability to reduce costs overall by scaling up and down (or completely stopping) computing resources in the cloud when they're not currently required.

Bandwidth

There is one major area where costs can actually increase, and this is in **bandwidth charges**. The network connection between on-prem data centers typically has a fixed installation and monthly cost independent of actual data transfer. In the cloud, by contrast, *outgoing* bytes between Availability zones (AZs) and regions are charged by the gigabyte. But *incoming* bytes to the cloud regions are free. This means that a `mongos` or a secondary node in the cloud is mostly reading data and will not be expensive in terms of bandwidth costs. No major cloud providers charge for bandwidth *inside* each availability zone but do charge a small fee for bytes between data centers in the same region.

Figure 8-6 shows a replica set with two members in two different on-prem data centers. There is a third member in the cloud, and a hidden nonvoting member in a different AZ in the same cloud region. Replication traffic to secondaries in the cloud is *incoming* data from the point of view of the cloud provider. Write traffic from a cloud-based `mongos` router to a primary on-prem is *outgoing* from the cloud provider's perspective and so will be charged.

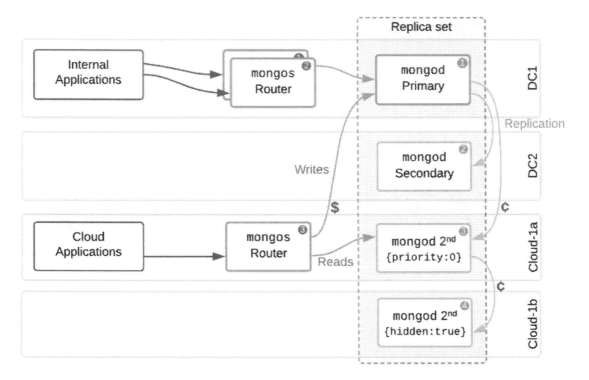

Figure 8-6. *An example hybrid deployment showing expensive bandwidth*

Many cloud providers also include an initial tier where a certain number of terabytes per month are free. The figures in Table 8-2 try to estimate pricing for an average MongoDB cluster. Prices will naturally drop over time, but the ratio between outgoing and the intra-region and intra-zone charges help explain why a replica set within the same zone can generally be cheaper.

Remember: Deploying all members of a replica set in a single AZ should be avoided since it skips a level of redundancy should that AZ suffer downtime.

Table 8-2. *Comparison of bandwidth charges (all prices in USD per GB)*

	Internal outgoing traffic		
	Outgoing cost per GB	**Between regions**	**Between AZs**
Microsoft Azure	$0.09	**$0.09** (same rate as outgoing to any other destination)	$0.01
Google Cloud	$0.13	$0.01 (within US) up to $0.08 (intercontinental), topping out at $0.15 to/from Oceania	$0.01
Amazon EC2	$0.09	$0.02	$0.01
IBM Cloud	$0.09	$0.09	-
Other (e.g., Linode, DigitalOcean)	$0.02	$0.02	-

Note   None of the listed hosting solutions charge for incoming traffic.

Compression

In modern MongoDB clusters, *intra-cluster communication* is already compressed to minimize bandwidth required, and this also has the pleasant side-effect of minimizing bandwidth charges when some data-bearing nodes are eventually moved to the cloud. Compression of traffic *between the app and the cluster* (mongos or primary) must be explicitly enabled via the compressors URI parameter or equivalent setter.

High availability

In many cases, organizations have access to two data centers, often designated Primary and disaster recovery (DR) sites. As we've already learned, a two-location topology doesn't assure high availability should one data center go offline, or be partitioned.

In these cases, some organizations chose to place an arbiter in the cloud to ensure that a data-bearing member can be elected primary in the remaining data center. However, any application using write concern majority (see Chapter 5) will stall if either data-bearing member is unavailable.

The best option is to keep full data-bearing nodes in the cloud and encrypt all communications and storage at rest. By optimizing write and update workloads to minimize the oplog, we keep the bandwidth charges for replication low.

Data sovereignty

We also need to consider the *location* of data-bearing nodes when moving to the cloud. Corporate policy or industry regulation may require that the "source of truth" physically reside on servers fully controlled by the organization and therefore on-prem.

Stale reads

In some cases, we can lower costs by reading somewhat stale data that has already been replicated to a secondary node in the Cloud. This data could always be several seconds delayed but could fall further behind during periods of high write workloads. (See the section of secondary reads for more.)

In any case, the nature of distributed systems with asynchronous replication means that we can never guarantee that a secondary has data that has already been written to the primary. The secondary just can't know what writes the primary has acknowledged but not yet flushed to disk.

As a result, **if you need to read the latest data, you must read from a primary** and incur any related bandwidth charges.

Migration steps

Let's imagine that we plan to start migrating our fully on-prem application and cluster to the cloud to build institutional knowledge and expertise in managing cloud infrastructure in advance of a complete move.

For this example, we'll assume a two-shard cluster in only two data centers, so part of the motivation for this migration is to add a third data center in the cloud. The other is to move some of the application servers to cloud infrastructure that can be scaled up and down each day during peak workloads (Figure 8-7).

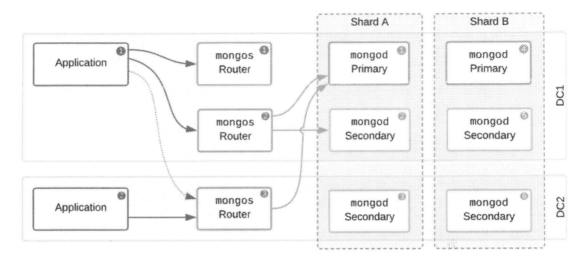

Figure 8-7. *Initially both data and applications are on-prem*

Cloud secondaries

If we are moving gradually to the cloud, we have a few different options as first steps. One (shown in Figure 8-8) is to keep the application on-prem initially and move some secondaries to the cloud. With *replication chaining* enabled by default, these nodes will replicate from either of the other nodes in their replica set in DC1 or DC2. By setting the priority to 0, we will ensure that these nodes never become primary in their sets. With primary nodes in the cloud, all applications' write traffic from DC1 and DC2 would be routed to the cloud, and replication traffic would come back, increasing cloud bandwidth costs significantly.

In a cloud-secondary topology, bandwidth charges will apply to outgoing heartbeats, but not incoming oplog data which is free.

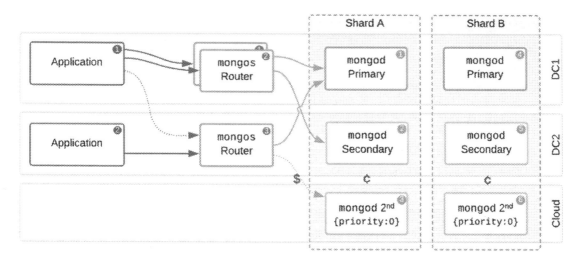

Figure 8-8. *Secondaries provide a third location for high availability, but applications remain on-prem*

Cloud applications

Another first step is to move some applications to the cloud, to save money by scaling back applications during downtime (see Figure 8-9). At this phase, we would normally see internal applications remain on-prem. These could be write-heavy *extract, transform, and load* (ETL) workloads from legacy systems, as well as internal analytics query workloads, among others.

As our best practice, we have placed mongos routers in the same region/zone as our application and microservices.

In this topology, we see that we are paying for outgoing bandwidth from the mongos to the primary for write payload. The outgoing request packets for reads are usually small compared to the result data coming back to the cloud, making these cheap.

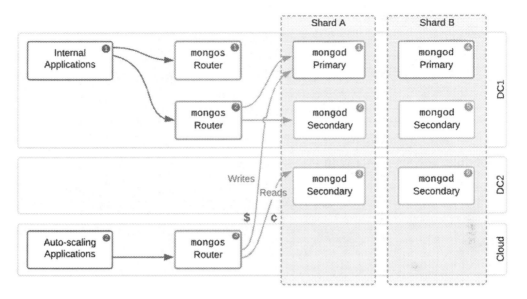

Figure 8-9. *Only auto-scaling applications are moved to the cloud*

Fully hybrid

The natural next step is to combine both applications and nodes in the cloud (see Figure 8-10). As before, the {priority: 0} ensures the cloud node is never primary since we assume the bulk of the writes will still originate from on-prem applications.

We incur bandwidth charges for any bytes from the cloud applications going out. However, in this case the client applications aren't writing much, and so the mongos and secondaries in the cloud are mostly *receiving* bytes which incur no charges.

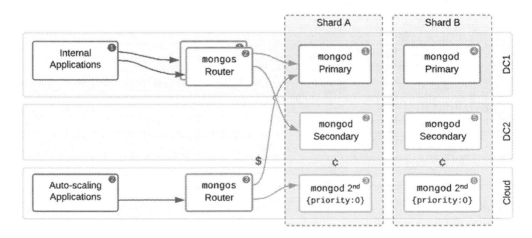

Figure 8-10. *A mixed topology allowing secondary reads in the cloud*

189

Asymmetric shards

The final iteration we'll explore includes asymmetric shards, with Shard A completely on-prem holding Shard A and Shard B mostly in the cloud but with at least one copy of all data on-prem (Figure 8-11).

By carefully "homing" certain databases on Shard A vs. Shard B, we can ensure that sensitive unsharded collections are fully on-prem. This can be useful when certain subsets of data cannot be stored in the cloud due to corporate policies or regulations.

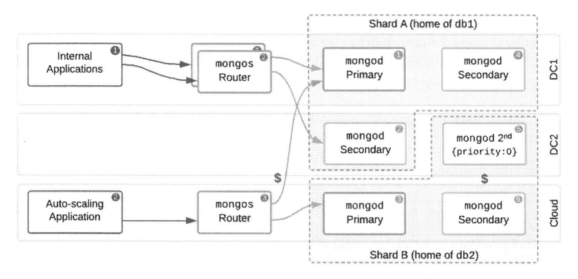

Figure 8-11. *An advanced topology with one shard primary in the cloud*

Note that we lose high availability in Shard A by having only two data centers. However, if DC2 is down, the internal applications would not actually be affected.

In the Cloud region, the two nodes could be placed in separate AZs to give the required redundancy.

Database structure

Figure 8-12 shows an example of how two databases could be deployed on our hybrid cluster. Shard A is physically located on on-prem data-bearing nodes, so while its sharded collections such as sharded1 will have half its data in Shard B and thus on cloud nodes, the unsharded collections (such as onprem1 and onprem2) are guaranteed to be stored on fully controlled on-prem hosts. By default, there is nothing preventing an application on the cloud with sufficient privileges from querying against `db1.onprem1` and transferring some confidential data over to the public cloud.

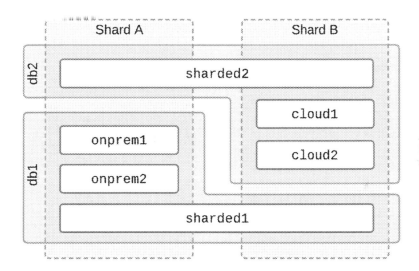

Figure 8-12. *Databases primarily for the cloud can be stored mostly in cloud*

A completely different alternative is to use the recent *field-level encryption* (FLE) mechanism (Chapter 4) which encrypts and decrypts certain fields or subdocuments inside the official drivers. This means that no confidential data ever reaches the database unencrypted, and therefore compliance rules requiring certain categories of data to be persisted only on-prem can be satisfied.

Access control

To fully prevent "leaking" of certain data, the applications on the cloud can connect with a user who only has read/write access to `db2` and so is not authorized to query the confidential data contained in `db1`.

In Listing 8-1, we define a user for each application. The user for the customer-facing application on cloud will not be allowed to access `db1`.

Listing 8-1. Create cloud user which can't read private db1

```
// The on-prem application user can access both databases
db.createUser(
```

```
  {
   user: "userPrem",
   pwd: "......"
   roles: [
     { role: "readWrite", db: "db1" }
     { role: "readWrite", db: "db2" }
   ],
  }
)
// The cloud application user can only access db2
db.createUser(
  {
   user: "userCloud",
   pwd: "......"
   roles: [
     { role: "readWrite", db: "db2" }
   ],
  }
)
```

You can further limit user accounts to connecting from specific IP addresses or CIDR ranges with authRestrictions[2] in MongoDB 3.6+. For example, the on-prem accounts could only be valid for login from on-prem address ranges. When dealing with highly confidential data, it's often simpler and safer to create two completely separate deployments that can each grow horizontally through sharding based on their individual data growth.

Custom write concerns

Let's imagine we have settled on our hybrid topology with two data-bearing nodes in private data centers and one in the cloud. We've prevented the cloud-based node from becoming primary, but our application isn't aware that the two on-prem nodes are special. Let's say that we want to guarantee that when we do an operation with write

---

[2]https://docs.mongodb.com/manual/reference/method/db.createUser/#authentication-restrictions

concern `majority,` the two on-prem nodes are the ones that acknowledge the write. In case one of the on-prem nodes goes down, the other can immediately take over the primary role without first having to catch up on the oplog.

MongoDB supports custom write concerns for this sort of use case. We will now create one called `OnPrem` which will ensure our nodes in `dc1` and `dc2` are always included.

First, we'd need to tag the nodes in each shard's replica set with a `dc` tag:

```
conf = rs.conf();
conf.members[0].tags = { "dc": "dc1"};
conf.members[1].tags = { "dc": "dc2"};
conf.members[2].tags = { "cloud": "aws-us-east1"};
rs.reconfig(conf);
```

Then we can create a custom write concern in each replica set:

```
conf = rs.conf();
conf.settings = { getLastErrorModes: { OnPrem : { "dc": 2 } } };
rs.reconfig(conf);
```

This creates a custom write concern called `OnPrem` which is satisfied *only* when the write is acknowledged on two members with *different* values of the `dc` tag.

Finally, the application can use this custom write concern as follows:

```
db.myCollection.update(
   { id: 123 },
   [ { $set: { value: "abc", lastUpdated: "$$NOW"} ],
   { writeConcern: { w: "OnPrem" } }
)
```

In our three-member shard, the `OnPrem` write concern means both nodes on-prem must acknowledge the write. If either on-prem node is unavailable, any write operations which specify this write concern will time out. Adding additional members in DC1 and DC2 and creating a PS|SS|S topology would provide better fault tolerance.

Internet of Things

The Internet of Things (IoT) has become a catchphrase for any sort of massively distributed system with many small devices, communicating over a network and usually collecting data for later collation and analysis.

There are numerous use case examples and blog posts for large-scale IoT services focusing on the required schema design, which are out of scope for this book. Typically, sensors and actuators communicate with edge gateways which do initial processing and aggregation of incoming data streams and prepare them for storage.

The main problem from a topology design perspective is the sheer number of connections required as shown in Figure 8-13. Most applications with MongoDB drivers will open a pool of connections to the database for reuse.

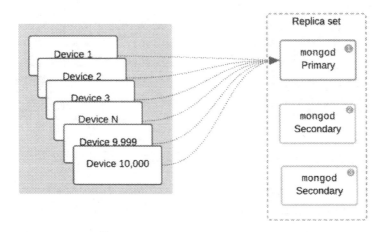

Figure 8-13. *IoT devices connecting directly to MongoDB*

Connection management

For applications running as *microservices*, this pool size (per service/pod/API) needs to be tuned right down to avoid overwhelming the primary node or mongos with open connections. In an Internet of Things scenario where there could be potentially millions of devices each connecting to a database to make updates, this problem is even worse.

Short-term connections

For IoT, the simple solution is to not maintain an open connection at all. Instead, build up a payload of data into a predefined bucket and only create the MongoClient object and establish a connection to the database once an hour (or even less frequently) to share a summary of that hour's data. Assuming this data can be inserted in a few seconds, several thousand devices would on average only open one connection to the cluster at any point in time.

Scaling writes

For millions of devices, you would probably need to consider sharded clusters. This would allow you to split up your data into subsets, each with a primary that can accept write operations. This allows scaling out for a high insert/update workload.

If you are expecting to deploy devices around the world and want to ensure low-latency write operations to MongoDB deployments, see Chapter 6 for more details on global topologies and Chapters 10 and 11 for advanced sharding topics.

In-memory storage

With the advent of the WiredTiger storage engine (default since 3.4), MongoDB also added a memory-only storage engine for Enterprise customers. The in-memory storage engine doesn't persist any data to disk and so is suitable for several niche use cases where predictable latency is important and data can be read and written purely in memory. When configured in a replica set, there's a low but nonzero risk that all nodes could fail simultaneously, resulting in complete data loss. Obviously, this is not suitable for any sort of system that needs to persist data in the long term. One solution is to deploy a fourth hidden node running the normal WiredTiger storage engine which persists data to disk (Figure 8-14). By keeping this in the same DC as the primary, we can ensure optimal replication performance by minimizing network latency.

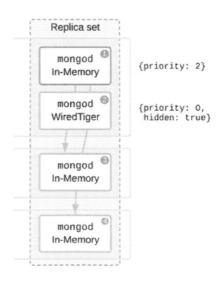

Figure 8-14. *An in-memory deployment with one WiredTiger node*

Since the in-memory storage engine doesn't flush data to disk, and so has almost no I/O requirements, it's tempting to assume that this engine can process data at a higher rather than a normal WiredTiger configuration. Interestingly, in most cases the throughput is almost identical, especially in replica sets where network latency makes replication the bottleneck.

Overall, while interesting, this storage engine isn't widely used as WiredTiger is similarly performant and keeps data persistent despite process or server restarts.

Mobile data-bearing nodes

The MongoDB replication system was designed as a distributed system with automatic failover. Writes always occur on the primary and are replicated. Sharding allows us to have multiple primary nodes to scale workloads, but each primary has a clear "scope" with no overlap and no risk of conflicts.

Certain use cases call for a type of master-master configuration where two isolated nodes both accept writes for the same range of documents, but which require a conflict-resolution mechanism.

In the following texts, we will explore one example of such a system: a mobile data-bearing node. By the end we will see that this approach is full of compromises.

Scenario

Let's imagine that we are running a motor racing team, and we need to move a complex set of equipment from site to site through a racing season. This kit will include a mobile rack of computing equipment and a MongoDB database. There is also a factory location where the rest of the team tests new equipment and scenarios, which also needs access to the same data.

Some of the racing locations will have a good Internet connection, and others may have no Internet connectivity at all.

As we move from race to race, the mobile computing kit may be offline for several weeks at a time. During these periods, the database in the factory needs to be online, available, and modifiable.

To make matters more difficult, the mobile database is a critical component of the race preparation, so any downtime is not acceptable. We'll therefore actually carry around two data-bearing nodes for redundancy.

So the question is: How can we design a topology that gives high availability, with two nodes being offline most of the time and allowing writes from two locations?

Solution

We'll walk through a number of examples to better understand the difficulty of these requirements. In Figure 8-15 we see a simplistic solution which includes two nodes in the mobile "kit" on different hosts to add a level of redundancy and a single node in the factory. Notice that the factory node has no priority and so will not become primary. In the mobile kit, one node has lower specs (CPU cores, memory) to save on resource costs and is given a lower priority so it normally stays as a secondary.

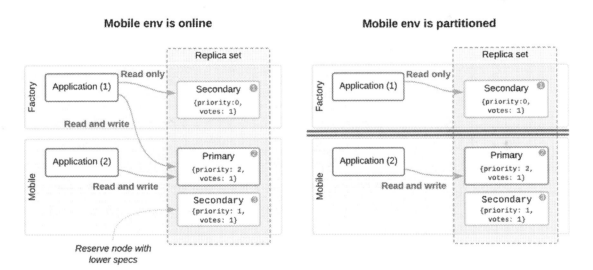

Figure 8-15. *A simplistic approach with a mobile kit*

When the mobile environment is online, we have a pretty standard replica set except that we are forcing one mobile node to be primary. This means that the factory location can write when the mobile kit has Internet connectivity, but can only read data otherwise (see Figure 8-15, right).

Fixed site redundancy

While we have mobile redundancy, we cannot afford to even read downtime in the factory, so we'll add a second data-bearing node in the factory. We have to add an arbiter to give us an odd number of members. We'll add the arbiter in the mobile kit so that it hosts a majority when the two environments are partitioned (due to no Internet).

Figure 8-16 shows this new five-member topology which has the same limitations for the factory when the two are partitioned or the mobile kit is powered down.

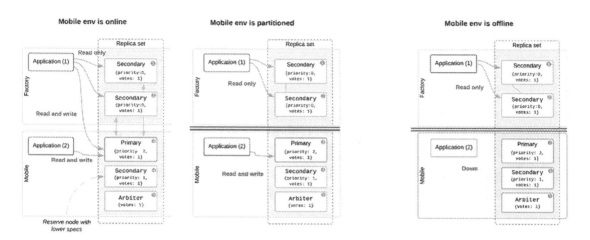

Figure 8-16. *A more complex mobile deployment with redundancy*

Multi-master

Now we want to integrate our requirement for a multi-master replica set. At least the factory needs to be able to write data temporarily while the mobile environment is partitioned. In Figure 8-17, we have restructured our topology to keep an arbiter in the factory and give one node a low priority. Now when the two are separated, an election will take place and node 1 in the factory will become the primary automatically. In the mobile environment some manual intervention is required to force a primary. We either use `rs.reconfig()` to remove the entry for the factory arbiter or create a new entry for a mobile arbiter. One risky approach would be to make an edit to `/etc/hosts` on all mobile hosts that overrides the factory arbiter's hostname to one running on a mobile kit host. Since the arbiter has no state or any data, a `mongod` process running in the mobile environment can easily take over this role.

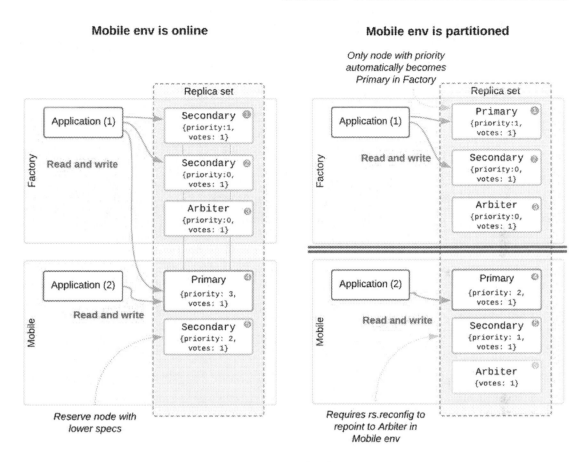

Figure 8-17. *A mobile deployment which facilitates multi-master*

Now, we have successfully forced a multi-master setup and created a *split-brain cluster*, although the election term mechanism should prevent one of them from accepting conflicting writes.

At this point, if the Internet were restored and the remapping of arbiter hostnames was reset, we would have inconsistent data on the nodes in the two environments possibly with completely different documents sharing the same _id primary key value. To avoid corrupting the replica set, and restoring stable replication, one set of nodes (either #1 and #2, or #4 and #5) would need their data files wiped and an initial sync initialized.

In reality, this master-master topology will require manual reconfiguration. Data loss will occur when the replica set is reunified. MongoDB Realm will offer toolkits for implementing offline mobile devices and automatic conflict resolution that might satisfy many use cases like this one without any cluster-level customizations.

Key takeaways

From this chapter, the key concepts to remember are as follows:

- While MongoDB does support a number of custom configurations, most of these come with various trade-offs.

- As with most information technology challenges, custom solutions require balancing a set of compromises against business goals.

- Using external authentication with Kerberos or LDAP can be scaled with load balancing and enabling connection retries.

- Hybrid on-prem/cloud clusters can give some useful benefits such as application scaling while keeping private data off-cloud.

- Internet of Things' database storage scaling can be achieved by controlling and closing connections, as well as increasing write capacity through sharding.

- Handcrafted master-master topologies are full of compromises and difficult to make resilient. MongoDB Realm introduces a production-ready syncing and conflict-resolution system.

CHAPTER 9

Backups and Restores

This chapter covers backup decisions related to topology design. We look at MongoDB's own enterprise tools for performing point-in-time restores of sharded clusters, to using scripts to snapshot geographically distributed clusters and retaining backup data in the same country of origin to comply with GDPR.

Goals

What are the primary motivations for taking backups? The following are some of the most commons real-world uses of backups:

- Roll back a change made due to *developer* error. This is might be an application error that was missed in testing and which started corrupting data at the entire deployment level.

- Roll back a change made due to *customer* error. There could be a customer in a multi-tenant system who deleted some data and then realized that it was still needed. This can sometimes be just a single database or collection that should be restored.

- Roll back a change made due to *administrator* error. A DB admin may has accidentally dropped an entire collection, thinking that they were connected to a test/staging cluster.

- There was a site-wide disaster and the production databases and all servers have been completely lost. In this case, an offsite backup is critical to restore operations.

- The latest backup of the production system is used to update a staging or development database so that testing can be done on real, recent data.

© Nicholas Cottrell 2020
N. Cottrell, *MongoDB Topology Design*, https://doi.org/10.1007/978-1-4842-5817-0_9

In all the preceding cases, the backup needs to reflect a consistent state of the database. We don't want to capture a snapshot of the data files where a write was partially flushed to disk, or when a write operation was partially complete.

Most organizations will define a *recovery point objective* (RPO) and a *recovery time objectives* (RTO) to ensure business continuity. The RPO is how much time of data changes may be lost. If we take backup snapshots every 12 hours, then the most recent 12 hours is the most that could be lost. The RTO is the maximum time allowed from a disaster occurring to when the database can be restored to full function from a backup. Certain backup/restore approaches will allow for much faster restoration than others.

Avoiding restores

While it is critical to have backups and to be able to restore large, geographically distributed sharded clusters, it will always be complex to bring them back online after a disaster. We should avoid human error contributing to such activities wherever possible.

Testing environments

One way to reduce errors is to have thorough unit and integration testing of the application. From a topology perspective, we can help by having proper development (DEV) and user acceptance testing or staging (UAT) environments. These should closely match the production (PROD) environments in terms of operating system version and security configuration and use the same MongoDB versions as production.

Both DEV and UAT can have less capacity in terms of CPU and memory resources, and the size of test data should be scaled down in a similar ratio from PROD. The UAT environment should match production topology at least in terms of the number of shards, config servers, and how collections are sharded.

For example, as shown in Table 9-1, if you have a PROD cluster with 6TB of data in three shards, each host having 256GB RAM, you could create a UAT environment with three shards but only 64GB of RAM per host, and 1/4 the amount of data, so about 1.5TB. This should keep a similarly proportional working set in memory to more closely match performance impact.

Table 9-1. *An example of scaled UAT and DEV based on PROD sizing*

	Topology	Resources	Data
PROD	3-shard cluster	32 cores, 256GB RAM per host	6TB total
UAT/Staging	3-shard cluster	8 cores, 64GB RAM per host	1.5TB total
DEV	single-shard cluster	8 cores, 32GB RAM per host	250GB total (1/3 shards, and 1/2 RAM of UAT)

Note   If you need to achieve very specific performance targets in production, the UAT environment should match resources exactly and restore recent backups to use real data in performance testing.

Catching application errors

DEV environments can be more simplistic in terms of sharding and redundancy. You could potentially have only a single-shard with a three-node replica set even when PROD is a multi-shard cluster with five-node replica sets.

DEV should be able to simulate both replica-set failovers and interactions with a `mongos`, so a standalone node is not sufficient. By testing application changes first in DEV, it should be possible to pick up bugs which could corrupt or delete valid data and avoid the need for cluster-wide rollbacks via a restore from backup.

Catching configuration errors

Major cluster changes like sharding new collections and adding indexes and any sort of configuration changes are prone to risks and so should first be run in UAT. By having the same number of shards in UAT, a database administrator can test shard tags, zoning, pre-splitting, and migration impact in an environment functionally identical to PROD.

Non-sharded clusters

Backing up of single-node or single replica sets is relatively straightforward since there is a single node taking writes. Sharded clusters are more complex since there are multiple primaries accepting writes, and chunks of documents may be migrated between shards at any moment.

Note   As we discussed in Chapter 1, a standalone node should never be used in production since it provides absolutely no resilience. However, there are cases where MongoDB is being used for local development or research, and in those cases, you may want to take a snapshot of the data at a particular point in time.

There are three general approaches for simple backups that apply to standalone nodes or replica sets:

1. **Stop the node**, and take a copy of all files in the data path, which could take minutes or hours.

2. **Lock the node** with db.fsyncLock(), and take a filesystem snapshot which requires a logical volume system like LVM and then unlock after a few seconds.

3. Keep **all nodes online**, and run mongodump to take a copy of the data, metadata (but not the indexes themselves), and the oplog.

Full copy

A full copy with the node stopped is the simplest and fastest to restore. If you have sufficient disk space to take a full copy of the dbpath, you will have a snapshot of all data and indexes. If you ever need to roll back to that point in time, you can launch a new mongod process with the --dbpath parameter pointing to this data and you have an instant restoration.

Since the data files are already compressed by default, any additional compression of this copy is unlikely to give noticeable additional space savings and will only require more time to decompress at restore time, further delaying the restoration.

Taking snapshots

The next approach is to take a clean filesystem snapshot. This approach requires a storage volume using the Linux *Logical Volume Manager* (LVM). With LVM, you can build a large volume group (VG) backed by multiple smaller physical volumes, optionally with a RAID level that gives some additional performance and redundancy. Then you can define a logical volume for your MongoDB node's data path, leaving some unallocated space that can be used for snapshots.

LVM allows you to take snapshots of the volume. You can take multiple incremental snapshots over time, with only the changed blocks (known as the delta) requiring storage space. You could keep 6-hourly or daily snapshots of a node requiring only a fraction of the physical storage space as taking full independent copies.

This same concept is used by *Elastic Block Store* (EBS) snapshots on Amazon AWS. Similar snapshots are also available on all major cloud providers. EBS snapshots are stored in the same cloud region as the original storage volume. If you have created a geopolitically sharded cluster to abide by global data protection regulations, your snapshots of customer data will naturally reside within the same country/region as the live data. You should still encrypt cloud backups to further ensure that GDPR and other regulation's duty of care clauses are satisfied. See Chapter 4 for more details on legal regulations.

Flush disks

The prerequisite step in MongoDB prior to taking a snapshot is very simple. You need to connect to the node via Mongo shell or a script and issue `db.fsyncLock()` before initiating the snapshot. This ensures that any pending disk flushes are made, and the state on disk is perfectly clean, just as if you had performed a clean shutdown of the node. However, at this point MongoDB is locked for any new write operations, so we want to avoid this for even very short periods in a production environment.

Trigger snapshot

Next, the snapshot can be triggered (but not necessarily completed), and then you can immediately issue `db.fsyncUnlock()` with the same Mongo shell. This removes the locks and allows writes again. Both LVM and EBS snapshots can then complete in their own time since they will reflect the point in time when the snapshot was triggered and the MongoDB data files were in a clean state.

Restoring snapshots

The major downside of this approach is that **restoring data files can be slow**. Since we are taking incremental backups to save space, restoring a particular snapshot requires combining the original state with the change deltas. Depending on the exact system you use, how often you trigger backups, and how frequently you update old documents, this could take anywhere between minutes and hours for terabytes of data.

If you are relying on these backups as a disaster recovery method, you need to perform realistic testing of the restore times to ensure that you can retrieve a recent backup within the required internal service-level agreement (SLA) time such as an RTO.

mongodump

When it's critical to never lock a node from writes, or there is no possibility to use LVM snapshots or similar, you can dump the entire data of a node (or entire cluster) using the mongodump command-line tool. This tool connects to a node and loops through all databases and collections, dumping out every document. By default, it creates a dump folder with a BSON-format data file for each collection and a corresponding metadata file containing the specification of any indexes. Note that for speed and compactness, **it does not dump the indexes themselves**. This can make the restore very slow as all indexes need to be rebuilt from scratch. Since a dump requires all documents to be loaded off disk and unpacked into memory, there will be considerable impact on the cache and consequently the overall database performance until the dump completes.

Oplog consistency

The dump of an entire node can take many minutes, and sometimes hours. You should optionally dump a copy of the oplog and apply that when restoring so that you get a consistent version of the data for a point in time. Otherwise, you may have dumped collection aaa first at time 0 (t^0), but at time point 5 minutes into the dump (t^5), the application made changes to documents in collection aaa and zzz. The final dump would include the change at t^5 to zzz but not aaa, giving an inconsistent state. The --oplogReplay option in mongorestore allows you to restore all collections consistently to the time that the mongodump completed with the --oplog option.

Data subsets

If the total database is simply too large, or you need to dump separate subsets of the cluster's data to different storage regions to facilitate GDPR compliance, you can use the `--query` option in `mongodump` to filter data. For example, if you want to dump EU data for the `customers` collection, you could dump with the following command:

```
mongodump -d=myDB -c=customers --query='{ "country":
  { "$in": ["BE", "CZ", "DK", "DE", "EE", ...] }}'
```

Read preference

By default, `mongodump` will read data from primary nodes to ensure the most recent data is dumped. But if you want to limit the performance impact on both storage I/O and flushing out the working set cache, you can specify `--readPreference=secondary` to force the data to be read from a secondary instead.

Mongorestore for dumps

When it's time to restore a dump generated by `mongodump`, the `mongorestore` command will connect to a cluster (empty or not) and can restore the data, optionally dropping any existing collections before importing.

Once the documents are restored, this command reads the metadata containing the index definitions and proceeds to create indexes. Depending on the complexity of the index, the distribution, and the size of the data, this **index build can take hours or days** to fully complete. During this time, application operation performance will be severely impacted. This long restore time is the major drawback of the `mongodump`/`mongorestore` approach for any large datasets.

Restoring a dump to standalone

When taking filesystem snapshots of sharded clusters, you must necessarily restore to a cluster with the same number of shards. With `mongodump`/`mongorestore` you can dump a sharded cluster into a unified backup set with one BSON file per collection. Then you can restore into a replica set or even a standalone node. This can be useful for updating DEV and UAT environments with real production data from a sharded cluster.

Replica sets

Backing up a replica set can be performed by any of the methods listed earlier for standalone nodes. However, we now have the choice of several nodes from which to take the backup. The primary is the node that has the very latest writes, but we don't want to block writes on the primary since it will affect any applications in production. A secondary is often a better choice for manual backups since if applications are reading from primary anyway (the default), they have no other external workload apart from replication. Even better is to add an additional hidden member for backups and other special workloads. We can safely call `db.fsyncLock()` or cleanly shut down this hidden node for extended periods without affecting the replica set availability or application performance in any way.

Delayed members

We introduced the concept of delayed members back in Chapter 2. For certain situations, these nodes could be used as additional protection against catastrophic human error. With no other backup available, if a database administrator accidentally dropped an entire collection, or removed a field from every document, this delayed member would at least have a consistent copy from some hours ago.

Should disaster happen and the live members have replicated the data removal, they could be shut down, the primary's oplog dumped, and the delayed member restarted configured as the primary. Figure 9-1 shows that the oplog could be *replayed* through the new primary until the moment before the faulty operations were performed.

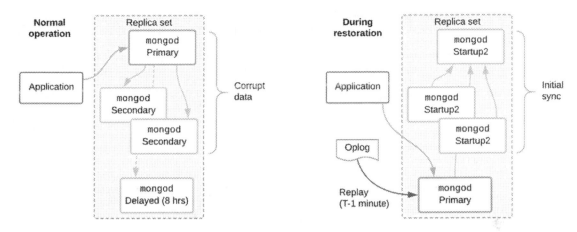

Figure 9-1. *Restoration via a delayed member*

Most human errors will not require such extreme measures. The delayed member can also be used to find and export a subset of data that was accidentally dropped or modified.

If you chose this approach, you should have a playbook and scripts pre-created and thoroughly tested so that the restore scenarios can be performed as smoothly as possible with little or no manual steps involved.

Note   In MongoDB Atlas or with Ops/Cloud Manager backups, you can utilize *queryable backups* to query a point in time in the continuous backup and look up an old document or value.

Restore performance

It's important to test, measure, and optimize restore performance as part of any disaster planning. To minimize any downtime, we want to keep backups physically close to the hosts that will be involved in any restore. When hosting on-prem, you will need to balance the requirement of keeping backups off-site, but close enough that network performance doesn't delay data downloading.

Shard size

One reason that the recommended maximum shard size is 2TB is because after this point restoring data hits the capacity limits of most networks. For example, if we attempt to replace a single 8TB node via a gigabit connection (in reality ~100 MB per second), this would take approximately 23 hours just for the data transfer time.

Cloud hosting

The major cloud providers all include a low-cost, long-term file storage solution suitable for storing large MongoDB backups. They generally do not publish benchmarks let alone guarantees for storage transfer speeds. Restore times will depend on the network in between, with compute instances in the same AZ and region being much faster than transferring to a private data center. Remember that restoring data from cloud storage will also incur bandwidth charges.

Media types

As we covered in Chapter 1, different media will have drastically different throughput rates. Simply copying or downloading large data files will not be highly dependent on seek times, so a spinning disk might not be drastically slower than an SSD. But when restoring via `mongorestore` and building indexes, the lower seek times of SSD could drastically reduce the overall restore time.

Compression

When restoring from a `mongodump`, the documents are stored in BSON format already and can be compressed on disk to reduce storage requirements by using the `--gzip` and `--archive` options. When restoring, there will be considerable CPU cycles required for decompression.

Index rebuilding

The associated `.metadata.json` file contains collection options and index definitions, and for each collection, the indexes will be rebuilt. Depending on the number and complexity of indexes, the distribution of field values, and the amount of RAM available, the index build stage could take as long or longer than the entire data writing stage.

Sharded clusters

Sharded clusters are much harder to consistently back up than replica sets because there are multiple primaries each performing writes, and which might be under various degrees of load. The secondaries will likely suffer from these same workload disparities. Figure 9-2 shows a global sharded cluster with individual backups for each shard being stored in the same region, but with the config servers data backed up to the *Americas* data center.

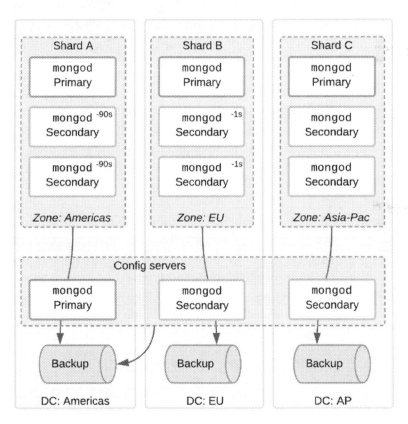

Figure 9-2. *A sharded cluster being backed up for GDPR compliance*

Replication lag

In the example above, a secondary from Shard A may be lagging its replication by 90 seconds due to a huge load, while Shard B secondaries are only 1 second behind their respective primaries.

Taking a backup from differently lagging secondaries would cause different amounts of acknowledged (but not replicated) writes to be missed in the backup. But backing up from primaries requires locking which would block writes and is also not acceptable in production.

Config servers

The config servers also need to be backed up. They contain the metadata about which shard should contain documents in a particular shard key range. This configuration needs to be restored also, so a three-shard cluster can only really be restored back into a three-shard cluster, unless a single unified mongodump has been performed through a mongos.

Pending chunk migrations

At the same time, there may be chunk migrations between the replica sets as part of shard balancing operations. A chunk of documents may exist on both the donor and recipient shards during migration, only to be cleaned off the donor shard later.

To ensure sharded clusters back up consistently, we need to both stop all balancing migrations and lock the config server primary and the primary from each shard to flush all writes to disk before taking filesystem-level copies or LVM snapshots.

Remember that if you want to snapshot from secondaries, you could temporarily pause the application's writes for a few seconds to allow secondaries to catch up before snapshotting. Both options will require the application to pause writes for a short period.

Geographic sharding

Each shard replica set may exist inside a geopolitical container which limits the transfer of data, including those being kept in encrypted backups. In order to avoid violating GDPR or other data protection regulations, we need to keep customer data in the same region. This has a positive benefit in that it reduces latency and likely increases throughput at restore time.

The only concern is that metadata from the config server chunk boundaries may leak into the config backups. For safety, it's best to store config server backups in the country with the most rigorous regulations.

Backup steps for snapshots

We will now walk through the backup details to fully understand the complexity that is involved. To take a consistent snapshot of a sharded cluster, the following steps must be followed.

Stop background operations

The balancer must be **disabled and inactive** before taking the snapshot. You can do this by connecting to a `mongos` and running `sh.stopBalancer()` and then waiting for any current migrations to complete. It may take a few minutes for any ongoing migrations to cleanly complete. When `sh.getBalancerState()` returns `false`, the balancer is now fully inactive and you can continue to the next step.

Shards and config

As you are taking a separate snapshot of each shard and the config server replica set, these snapshots are necessarily separated in time. If any write operations are still active in the sharded cluster, those operations may not have been flushed to disk when you take the snapshots. To ensure a valid and consistent backup of the entire sharded cluster, it is important to stop **all writes** to the cluster and **flush all data** to disk using the `db.fsyncLock()` method before taking any snapshots.

Snapshot from primary

For every **shard** in the cluster, connect to the current primary node with a Mongo shell connection and run `db.fsyncLock()`. Keep this connection open in a separate window so that we can unlock the node again easily.

Then connect to the primary of the **config server** replica set, and run the same `db.fsyncLock()` command, keeping the window open.

This step will block primaries temporarily from accepting writes from applications. It will appear to applications that the primary has suddenly stopped responding to any communication. It's important that this should only be run during designated off-peak backup periods.

Now **trigger the filesystem snapshot** via LVM or the cloud provider storage snapshot via the UI or API. Once the snapshot is triggered, you do not need to wait until it completes fully.

We should now run `db.fsyncUnlock()` on the config server first and then all shards, in the reverse order that we locked.

Snapshot from secondary

If you want to avoid blocking applications from writing even for a few seconds, you could choose to instead take snapshots from secondaries.

This option can produce an *inconsistent* backup because secondaries replicate asynchronously. Figure 9-3 shows a cluster with Shard B being less loaded, and consequently it has less replication lag (5–10 seconds, vs. 80–90 seconds on *Shard A*). First *Write 1* is performed against Shard A and acknowledged. Then *Write 2* is performed on Shard B. When a snapshot is taken 10 seconds later, the second write will be recorded in the backup, but Write 1 which happened first will not appear in this same backup snapshot.

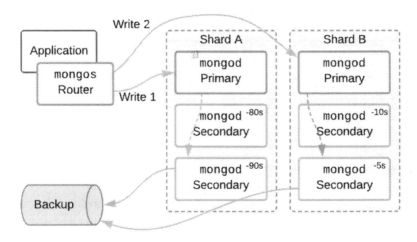

Figure 9-3. *An inconsistent sharded cluster backup from secondaries*

Best practices are already that you use write concern `majority`. This will ensure that recent writes are replicated to at least one of the secondaries. You can connect to the current primary of each shard replica set and run `rs.printSlaveReplicationInfo()` to set a report of how many seconds each secondary is behind in replication. By choosing a time of day with very little write activity on the cluster, when the secondaries are able to replicate immediately, you are more likely to get consistent snapshot of the entire cluster.

The procedure for secondaries is almost the same as earlier for primaries. Lock the **shard secondaries** instead, but still the config server **primary,** and then unlock them in the reverse order.

Restore normal operations

Now that all snapshots are complete and all nodes are unlocked, you can re-enable the balancer again by connecting to any `mongos` and running `sh.setBalancerState(true)`.

Restore steps from snapshots

Restoring a sharded cluster from filesystem snapshot manually is also a complex procedure. The key points for the restore phase are as follows.

Shut down the cluster

Since we will be replacing the data files on disk from a restored version, it's important to fully shut down all `mongod` and `mongos` instances for the shards and config server replica sets.

Restore the config server

Restore the config server replica set **snapshot** first. This will differ depending on what kind of LVM or cloud configuration was used to make the snapshot. Normally you would mount the snapshot in a temporary mount point and then copy over the datafile replacing the files in the existing `dbPath`.

Then **start one** config server node as a standalone, by commenting out the `replSetName` and `clusterRole` from the configuration file.

Once that node is up, connect to it with the Mongo shell and drop the local database since this contains instance-specific data from the original node:

```
use local
db.dropDatabase()
```

When restoring over the top of the same cluster with same hostnames and node ports, no configuration changes are required. But if you are restoring into different hosts as part of a test, or to "lift and shift" an existing cluster, you will need to update the hostnames in the `config.shards` collection. It's important to follow the documentation carefully to get this correct.

It's now time to restart the config server replica set, starting with one node. First, **shut down** the mongod we started as standalone. Revert the `replSetName` and `clusterRole` settings by uncommenting those lines.

We effectively removed replica set config when dropping the `local` database. We should now initialize the replica set with

```
rs.initiate()
```

This creates a replica set with one member.

Now we can wipe the `dbPath` and start up the other config server nodes. We then add them into the set by using `rs.add(...)` on the already open Mongo shell connection:

```
rs.add("config2.bigDB.bigcorp.local:27019")
rs.add("config3.bigDB.bigcorp.local:27019")
```

They will then make a copy of the restored data via an initial sync.

Restore the shards

We now need to restore each shard's replica set. We follow the same steps as when restoring the config server set, except that in addition to dropping the local database, we need to create a temporary admin user to clean up some other metadata. We restart the mongod as a single-node replica set and add any additional members, allowing them to initial sync the data from the shard. Detailed steps are documented in the *Restore a Sharded Cluster*[1] online documentation.

Restore the mongos routers

Finally, start your mongos nodes and the newly restored sharded cluster should be ready to use.

---

[1]https://docs.mongodb.com/manual/tutorial/restore-sharded-cluster/index.html

Conclusion

Sharded cluster backups are complex but can be achieved with open source tooling. Human error is always a risk, so it's always better to develop playbooks or scripts which automate the process as much as possible. Both backup and restores should be **tested** on a regular basis to ensure that the system is working as expected and so that restores can be completed as quickly as possible should the need ever arise.

Ops/Cloud Manager

A much better approach to any of the preceding manual or custom solutions is to use the backup solutions built by MongoDB Inc. MongoDB Enterprise licenses include the possibility to use *Ops Manager* or *Cloud Manager*. The Cloud Manager backup service can also be bought separately. Both tools perform automated backups and support features including scheduled snapshots, point-in-time restores, and queryable backups. For replica sets, you can restore to any chosen point of time in the last 12–24 hours (depending on your chosen configuration) or use one of the daily, weekly, or monthly snapshots.

Point-in-time restores

This feature fully supports sharded clusters too. The backup system injects synchronized time markers into the backups of each replica set, allowing you to perform a **consistent** sharded cluster restore to a 15-minute granularity.

Newer versions of MongoDB and Ops/Cloud Manager leverage the native snapshotting ability of the WiredTiger storage engine and can save these snapshots into a S3-compatible block store. A copy of the oplog still needs to be kept in order to fill in the gap from the last snapshot until the exact time desired for the restore.

Other features

Even if you have a geopolitical sharded cluster, Ops Manager lets you back up each shard to a different location to ensure *compliance* as customer data never leaves its country of origin.

You can also launch a temporary cluster from a backup to perform *partial restores*. Queryable backups support ad hoc queries and export subsets of a point-in-time snapshot of the cluster. This makes it easy to restore a single collection or document.

Ops Manager gives a fast, cost-effective, and powerful restore mechanism which covers all major use cases and can be achieved with just a few steps in the UI.

Key takeaways

From this chapter, the key concepts to remember are as follows:

- Incremental copies of the entire MongoDB data path can be taken using a low-impact LVM snapshot feature. Cloud computing storage (like EBS volumes) also provide a similar snapshot feature.

- Backups of individual nodes can be taken via a `mongodump`, a filesystem-level copy, or snapshot as long as nodes are stopped or writes are flushed first.

- For GDPR compliance, backups should be kept in the same country as their source shards.

- Restoring from filesystem snapshots can often be slow due to bandwidth and reading from incremental copies.

- Restoring from a `mongodump` can also take a long time since indexes are not included in the dump and must be rebuilt after the data is restored.

- Backing up entire sharded clusters in a consistent state with community tools requires a temporary pause in the write-load.

- Sharded clusters can be backed up live with no workload impact using Enterprise tools like Ops and Cloud Manager.

- With Enterprise backup, replica sets can be restored to any point in time and sharded clusters to any 15-minute interval in time.

- Enterprise tools also allow queryable backups to restore just one collection or even a single document from a particular point in time.

CHAPTER 10

Advanced Sharding

In this chapter, we expand the discussion on sharding by planning for deployments with very large datasets or extensive write workloads. We review challenges for sharding in these cases and explore methods to avoid or mitigate problems as the data grows.

Since we are working with shards, all examples and commands shown in this chapter must always be run through a `mongos` instance and never directly on the shards themselves.

Indications for sharding

There are a few different options for scaling depending on the size of the data and the access patterns. If you have a "small" database of less than 2TB of data, then a replica set is normally the best topology since it avoids the overhead of sharded clusters.

If your application is *write-heavy* and you are seeing that the primary's input/output operations per second (IOPS) are exceeding the storage layer's capacity, then increasing the storage throughput is the best approach to scaling up. If the application is doing many *small random reads*, this can mean that there is not a clear working set, and in such situations the bottleneck can be both seek times on storage and also limited memory.

MongoDB will cache documents in memory, so if you have a certain set of common documents (in our ecommerce example this might be active shoppers and the list of the 10k most popular items in the shop), then the memory resources for the nodes should be sufficient to keep these documents in the memory cache.

Shard keys

As we discussed in Chapters 1 and 6, choosing the optimal shard key can be a difficult design decision in balancing the needs for equalized data distribution, minimizing balancing operations, and maximizing how queries can target a single shard as much as possible.

219

© Nicholas Cottrell 2020
N. Cottrell, *MongoDB Topology Design*, https://doi.org/10.1007/978-1-4842-5817-0_10

Hot shards

If your shard key is configured so that most inserts for a given point in time are all routed to the same one shard, then that shard is called the **hot shard**. Be careful to avoid hot shards because they hurt overall throughput and lead to problems with rebalancing.

Effects on throughput

Routing everything to a single shard removes all the benefits of a sharded cluster in that a single primary is processing all the write workload. Ideally, we want all writes (inserts, updated, and deletes) to be equally distributed to all shard primaries at all times.

In Figure 10-1, an application is inserting documents with auto-generated UUIDs which are based on the current time. As a result, all of them fall into the range of 533000001 to B200000 and are being sent to Shard B.

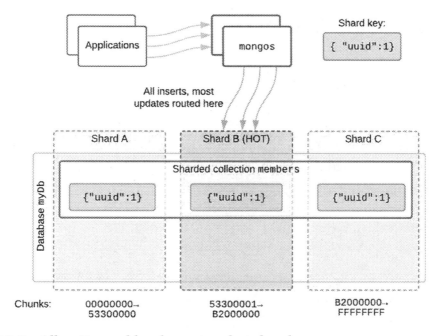

Figure 10-1. *All write workload goes to a hot shard*

Rebalancing effects

Not only does a hot shard slow down bulk import throughput, but it also requires these documents to be migrated elsewhere. As shown in Figure 10-2, for 300GB written to a hot shard, the balancer will need to read 200GB again from that shard in order to write 100GB to each of the other shards.

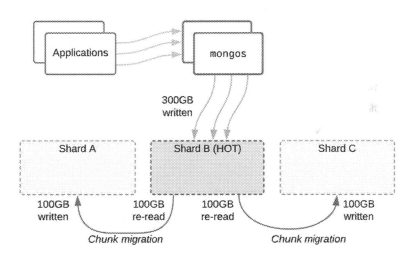

Figure 10-2. *Worst-case scenario when importing into a hot shard*

By writing once directly to each shard, the I/O impact is only writing 300GB in total, as opposed to 500GB writing and 200GB reading. Figure 10-3 shows this best-case scenario.

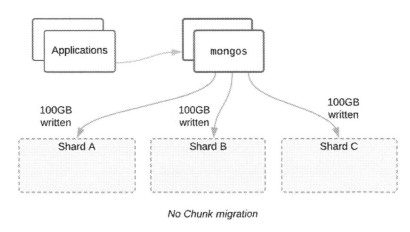

Figure 10-3. *Best case where each shard receives equal data with no migration*

Unique values

In all MongoDB collections, the `_id` field acts like a primary key and always has a corresponding index with a unique constraint. This prevents any two documents sharing the same `_id` value in a standalone or replica set. When sharding, it's important to understand that unique constraints are **local** to each shard. Imagine you created two unique indexes in your collection with

```
db.members.createIndex( { "userName": 1 }, { unique: true } )
db.members.createIndex( { "uuid": 1 }, { unique: true } )
```

and then sharded with one of those:

```
sh.shardCollection("myDb.members, { "uuid": 1}, true)
```

The third parameter in `shardCollection` here tells the sharding system to maintain a unique constraint on this shard key. So now we have ensured that `uuid` values are unique both within each shard and at the cluster level.

However, we have no such constraint on `userName` **at the cluster level**. Imagine that two new users signed up simultaneously from two different application servers and chose the **same** username. We would effectively see two inserts coming up through one or multiple `mongos` instances:

```
db.members.insertOne({ _id: ObjectId(...123),
    uuid: "0123-abcd...", userName: "logikewl", ...)
db.members.insertOne({ _id: ObjectId(...456),
    uuid: "4567-efab...", userName: "logikewl", ...)
```

As you can see, the auto-generated `_id` value and the application-generated `uuid` values are both unique as expected. Since we have sharded on `uuid`, it's quite likely that these two inserts are sent to different shards. Let's say the first goes to Shard A and the second to Shard B (see Figure 10-4). It's also likely that there is no other user with that username, and so both inserts succeed at the shard level, but we now have two `members` in our system with the same username.

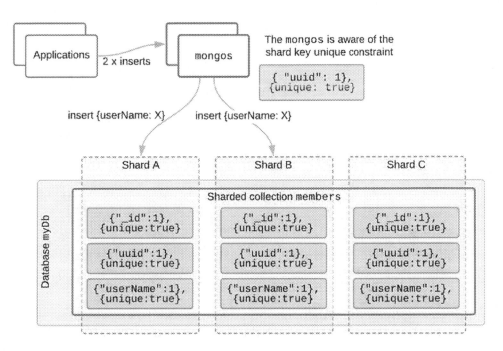

Figure 10-4. *Unique constraints at the shard level can be violated*

Note   The *highly* random nature of the ObjectId data types means that it is extremely unlikely for the preceding scenario to insert two documents with the same value for _id.

Shard keys and unique fields

When the shard key is something other than {_id: 1}, then you could get a situation where two documents have the same _id field and exist on different shards (since the unique constraint on the _id index is per shard).

Sharding on _id

The "primary" key field _id alone is not normally a good choice as the shard key. Using the *ObjectId* data type or a custom ID with ascending values for the _id field can lead to a hot shard. The first bytes of the ObjectID are a date/timestamp, and so even when generated from different application servers, they will have almost identical sort order.

While integer IDs are often ascending, if your application can generate UUID with a random prefix, the problem of hot shards can be avoided.

There are many better options such as using a hash of the ID (e.g., {_id: "hashed"}) which should distribute documents more evenly across the shards.

If you are almost always querying on other important fields, you could use a compound shard key like {country: 1, _id: 1} to benefit from shard targeting optimizations.

Nonunique shard key values

There is no requirement that shard keys should be unique, and no immediate performance concerns when multiple documents share a shard key.

The major concern about the same shard key value being shared by many documents is that eventually you could create a **jumbo chunk**. This is when a chunk is indivisible and larger than the max chunk size (64MB by default). The balancer will not migrate jumbo chunks due to the performance impact and it can eventually lead to unbalanced shards.

Time-based shard keys

Using a field that stores the *current* or *insert* date is a bad choice for a shard key because it is essentially incrementing. If you are sharding on a different date, like a customer's date of birth, this might not cause problems as long as documents are not bulk-loaded in this order.

Compound shard keys starting with the current date are also problematic when they are the first field in the key. So, a shard key like {insertDate: 1, custId: 1} is likely to lead to a hot shard. A key like {custId: 1, insertDate: 1} allows good shard targeting for queries filtering on custId, but monotonically ascending customer ID values would also create a hot shard.

Later in this chapter, we will explore some techniques for efficiently bulk loading data into sharded collections with pre-splitting.

Hashed shard keys

When sharding a collection as "hashed", use numInitialChunks to pre-chunk a collection to a certain number of chunks (say 1024). Let the balancer migrate these empty chunks first, before initializing the import workload.

As you load data, these chunks will be split as documents are added to ensure they stay under the chunk size limit. This splitting is a question of updating metadata in the config servers and doesn't actually require I/O on the shards themselves. Since the hash algorithm guarantees good distribution, in most cases there will be almost no chunk imbalances even after additional splitting, so no chunk migrations should be needed to restore balance between shards.

However, without sufficient cardinality of the original values, a hashed shard key will still lead to jumbo chunks and balancing problems.

Refining keys

Upcoming versions of MongoDB (4.4 and later) will allow refining an existing shard key by adding an additional field as a compound shard key. This can be useful if the current shard key is not selective enough and gives jumbo chunks that are otherwise too large to migrate.

Advanced splitting

In most cases and with a decent shard key choice, MongoDB's native behavior will automatically balance data while splitting active chunks and redistributing them across the shards.

Note   Whenever manipulating shard configuration or chunks, you should always first stop any balancing activity by running `sh.stopBalancer()`. After making changes, don't forget to restart the balancer again with `sh.startBalancer()`.

In the following sections, we'll explore a few cases where manual splitting is beneficial.

Split early

When you are about to load a large amount of data into MongoDB in a new collection, it's important to **pre-split** the collection before starting the load. This avoids the overhead of splitting and moving chunks during the operation. Documents will be inserted directly onto the final shard.

As balancing is calculated at the chunk level, it's important to define chunk ranges which will include approximately the same number of documents being loaded. We want to avoid creating chunks which will have no documents, since we'll end up with an unbalanced cluster in terms of bytes stored per shard.

In Figure 10-5 we see a cluster with 20 chunks on each shard. However, due to artifacts from the automatic splitting algorithm, chunks on the original Shard A tend to have slightly more documents per chunk, meaning that Shard A is 30% larger in terms of bytes.

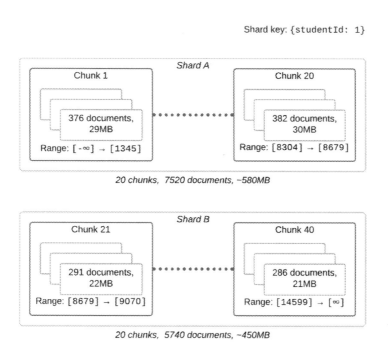

Figure 10-5. *Pre-splitting can create chunks with uneven distributions*

Manual splitting

If the shard key/value distribution is known in advance and we are not using a hashed shard key, then we can manually pre-split with a script.

Let's say we run a school system in which student ID numbers are assigned in ascending order. This is a not a good choice for single-field shard key, and we'll address some issues as part of this example.

The previous database contains 200,000 students, past and present, that we want to load. We will define 100 chunks, and each chunk will contain 2000 documents. We can use the following script to achieve that goal on an empty sharded collection students:

```
for (var i = 0;  i < 100; i++) {
  sh.splitAt("school.students", { studentId : 2000*i } );
}
```

If we immediately realize that the first student ID starts at 5000, we can safely merge in the first two adjacent empty chunks with

```
db.adminCommand( {
  mergeChunks: "school.students",
  bounds: [ { studentId : MinKey },
            { studentId : 6000 } ]
} )
```

Note that we cannot ever directly remove a chunk since the range of chunk definitions must span all the way from MinKey to MaxKey (essentially -infinity to +infinity).

Once the balancer has moved chunks around, we'll see chunks evenly distributed between the available shards, like the result from sh.status(true) shown in Listing 10-1.

Listing 10-1. Output of sh.status() showing newly distributed empty chunks

```
school.students
    shard key: { "studentId" : 1 }
    unique: false
    balancing: true
    chunks:
            shardA     34
            shardB     34
            shardC     33
    { "studentId" : { "$minKey" : 1 } } -->> { "studentId" : 0 } on :
    shardA Timestamp(2, 0)
    { "studentId" : 0 } -->> { "studentId" : 2000 } on : shardC
    Timestamp(3, 0)
    { "studentId" : 2000 } -->> { "studentId" : 4000 } on : shardB
    Timestamp(4, 0)
```

```
{ "studentId" : 4000 } -->> { "studentId" : 6000 } on : shardC
Timestamp(5, 0)
{ "studentId" : 6000 } -->> { "studentId" : 8000 } on : shardC
Timestamp(6, 0)
{ "studentId" : 8000 } -->> { "studentId" : 10000 } on : shardA
Timestamp(7, 0)
```

Now our previous mergeChunks command will fail since the chunks inside that range are located on different shards and can longer be easily merged.

Pre-split hashed shard key

If we want to ensure a good distribution, and we know that we will mostly filter with a particular studentId in all queries, we can shard on a hashed shard key and create 1024 initial chunks immediately:

```
db.adminCommand( {
   shardCollection: "school.students",
   key: { studentId: "hashed" },
   numInitialChunks: 1024
 } )
```

Note that any queries or aggregations filtering on a range of studentId values or not including studentId at all will hit **all** shards on every operation and will not benefit from the horizontal scaling of shards. For these common query patterns, hashed shard keys should be avoided.

Pre-split UUID

What if we need to pre-split on a UUID or other randomly distributed hexadecimal value? Each character in the UUID can be 0–9 and a–f, giving 16 different possible values.

Let's split our UUID range into 1024 chunks. To do that we need at least 3 hex digits ($16^2 = 256$ but $16^3 = 4096$) and we'll be putting them in the most significant digits (i.e., the 3 leftmost) for the ranges. The following script will create these chunks:

```
// Use a for loop for each digit
for ( var x=0; x < 16; x++ ){
  for( var y=0; y < 16; y++ ) {
  // For the innermost loop we will increment by 2 to get 2048 total
  iterations
    // We only use z=0,4,8,16
    for ( var z=0; z<16; z+=4 ) {
    // Now construct the UUID with zeroes for padding
    // toString method takes an argument to specify the base
        var prefix = "" + x.toString(16) + y.toString(16) +
            z.toString(16) + "00000000000000000000000000000";
        // The split command to creates the appropriate chunk
        db.adminCommand( { split : "school.students" ,
            middle : { _id : prefix } } );
    }
  }
}
```

Directing load

Pre-splitting gives one other aspect to control data flow. Since the chunks are defined before the import starts, you can quickly move around chunks and assign certain ranges of data to shards, either manually with moveChunk or via zone sharding (see Chapter 6 for more examples).

If you have *asymmetric shards* with one shard for recent data and other shards for historic data, then you can ensure that documents are imported directly onto their target shards with no further migration.

Bulk loading without pre-splitting

If you can't know the distribution of data in advance, there are a few tricks to efficiently bulk loading data that don't require manual pre-splitting.

Sample and balance

One approach is to import a small portion of the data until N chunks have been created. Now pause the import and let those chunks be migrated to the available shards by the balancer. If the sample was representative, when we resume the import we should have reasonably well-distributed shard load.

Randomize order

Bulk loading of data sorted by the shard key is guaranteed to give the worst possible performance, since the load will hit one shard at a time. One way to avoid that problem is to **randomize** the order of the data being imported with respect to the shard key. If you have chosen the shard key to optimize for reads and updates during the application lifetime, you can greatly reduce the data load phase by **not** loading data in ascending order.

If you can randomize the data that is exported from the legacy system or sort it by a different field (e.g., the student's last name rather than ID), then the load is more likely to send subsequent new documents to different shards, smoothing out the load on each shard and maximizing throughput.

Split existing shards

Imagine you have a two-shard cluster which is reaching the limit of its current computing resources, and it's taken a while to get permission to buy the necessary new hardware. We recently received approval to add two new shards. How can this be achieved efficiently?

Initial load

With a system under heavy load, the first few hours after linking the new shards into the cluster will be the most critical, as there is the existing application workload **plus** migration of chunks. The migration requires heavy *read* I/O on the donor shards, as well as heavy *write* I/O workload on the recipient shard primary, followed by heavy replication workload on the recipient secondaries.

Migration windows

If the initial migrations can be made during off-peak application workload, and in short windows, some of the pressure will be relieved on the original shards (See *Throttling balancing impact* below for more details). Over time, longer and longer migration windows can be used as the shards come closer to equilibrium.

Mitosis

In some distributed database systems, there is the concept of *mitosis* – splitting up an existing shard into two subsets. Unfortunately, this approach is not yet supported by current versions of MongoDB.

One option for doubling shards is to add the new shard hardware, and let the balancer handle the rebalancing of data via migration. As discussed in Chapter 6, each pair of donor/recipient shards can have a migration in parallel. So in this case there will be two parallel migration of chunks to the two new shards.

Managing balancing

Before you start making decisions about which collections will be sharded and with what keys, it's useful to first understand how data is actually balanced.

Primary shard

When sharding a cluster, you can have a combination of sharded and non-sharded collections. Each logical database has a single **primary shard** (completely unrelated to "primary" nodes) where all unsharded collections are homed.

In Figure 10-6, we see a sharded cluster with a single logical database db1 which has a number of collections. Only the largest collections bigColl1 and bigColl2 have been sharded, and their documents have been distributed equally across the shards based on chunks.

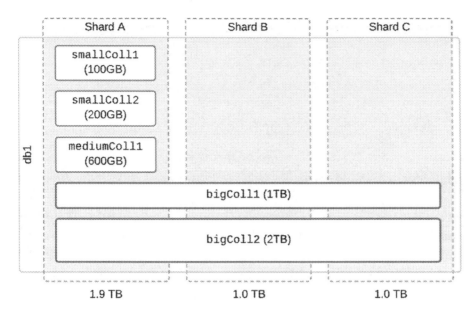

Figure 10-6. *A single database with some sharded collections*

Depending on the size of the non-sharded collections, you can get some considerably unbalanced shards. In this case, Shard A is almost twice the size of the other shards.

Rebalancing collections

So how do we deal with an unbalanced cluster such as when one shard is twice the size of the others? In some cases, the simplest option may simply be to give additional resources to hosts in Shard A. Additional CPU cores and memory should allow these hosts to handle the additional workload servicing requests to this unsharded collection. But we end up with a mix of host types which is complex to manage and scale.

We also don't want to shard very small collections since there is some extra overhead of balancing their data and managing the metadata for these collections. The worst downside, though, is that we'd have to route certain queries (that don't include the shard key) to *all* shards and perform *scatter-gather queries* which are as slow as the slowest shard at the time.

In this case, if we chose to shard mediumColl1, we would migrate 200GB of data from Shard A to each of Shard B and Shard C.

Move primary shard

In situations where you have multiple logical databases, MongoDB will automatically assign the primary shard for any new database to an undercommitted shard. However, if you started with just a single shard and added additional shards over time, the primary shards will **not** be automatically reassigned to the newer shards. You will have all unsharded collections homed on the original shard. An example is shown in Figure 10-7 where new shards have 400GB less data per shard.

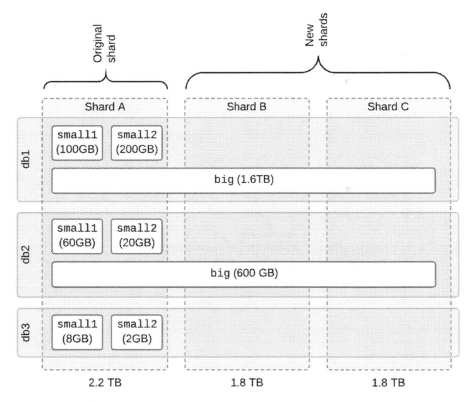

Figure 10-7. *An expanded cluster with unsharded collections on Shard A*

To manually rebalance the load of unsharded collections, you can use the `movePrimary` command to reassign the primary shard for a particular database to a shard of your choice. In the preceding example, this can be achieved with the following commands:

```
db.adminCommand( { movePrimary : "db2", to : "shardB" } )
db.adminCommand( { movePrimary : "db3", to : "shardC" } )
```

Additional shards

In Figure 10-8, we see a similar sharded cluster but with two logical databases. In this case, db1 has its primary shard on Shard C, and db2 has its primary shard homed on Shard A. There are three sharded collections: db1.bigColl1, db2.bigColl1, and db2.bigColl2.

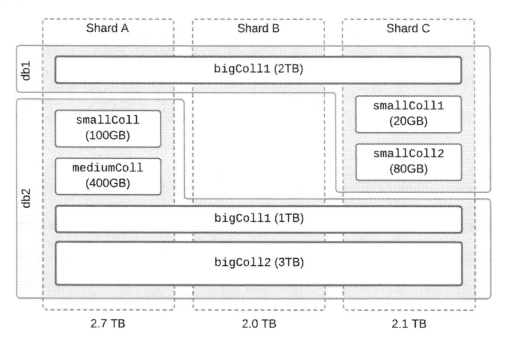

Figure 10-8. *A relatively well-balanced sharded cluster*

In this case, our Shard A is a slightly above the recommended threshold for shard data sizes, and we should consider adding an additional shard to this cluster. Should we do that, these three large sharded clusters will automatically be distributed evenly and approximately 0.5TB will be migrated from the current three shards, into the new fourth shard.

This migration process may take several days as it is given a low priority to ensure that migration doesn't impact normal application or replication traffic.

Throttling balancing impact

We need to plan and manage the chunk migration **workload** that is generated after adding a shard to ensure it doesn't have a negative effect on an already loaded cluster.

We should also be careful when adding shards on a nearly saturated **network** with limited free capacity, especially where bandwidth between data centers is saturated during business hours.

One simple approach it to use the **built-in balancer window**, which allows you to choose a fixed window every day to allow chunk transfers to occur.

For example, in Listing 10-2, we activate a daily window between 1 a.m. and 6:30 a.m. local server time every day of the week.

Listing 10-2. Activate the built-in balancing window

```
use config;
db.settings.update(
    { _id: "balancer" },
    { $set: { activeWindow :
        { start : "01:00", stop : "06:30" } } },
    { upsert: true }
)
```

Weekend workloads

Many applications have special weekend workloads. Some have almost no user traffic and could safely have the balancer running only on weekends. Others have special load and transform or analytics workloads and so want to avoid any balancing at all. For these cases, an external `cron` job or trigger can use a Mongo shell script to turn on and off the balancer at will:

```
mongo --uri mongodb://U:P@mongos1.bigcorp.local:27017/config
  --authenticationDatabase admin
  --eval "sh.startBalancer()"
```

The same approach can be used to stop the balancing with `sh.stopBalancer()`.

Note   From MongoDB 4.2 stopping the balancer will also halt autosplitting of chunks. This change effectively stops almost all write workload on the config server's replica set when balancing is stopped.

Managing storage

One of the biggest concerns for admins is ensuring that hosts for growing databases have sufficient storage space. Unexpectedly running out of space can lead to downtime and even data corruption.

Maximum storage size

In some cases, it can be useful to control the maximum amount of data per shard, allowing asymmetric shard sizes without having to control chunk ranges explicitly with zones. When adding new shards to an existing cluster, the new hosts will often have larger, faster storage devices. We want to avoid filling up older, smaller shards since running out of disk space risks data corruption and many other problems.

For example, we could set a maximum size of 1TB (1,048,576 MB) for our Shard A by running the following:

```
config = db.getSiblingDB("config")
config.shards.updateOne( { "_id" : shardA"},
    { $set : { "maxSize" : 1048576 } } )
```

The balancer will not consider any shard as a chunk recipient if doing so would exceed this configured maximum storage size.

Determining actual storage size

The actual size on disk will vary even between each member in a shard replica set. Members that have been recently initial synced or `compacted` may have significantly smaller real storage space used than nodes that have been running a long time which may have severely fragmented storage.

WiredTiger uses a no-overwrite algorithm which will not actually overwrite the old document version, but instead finds an unused block and reuses it. Deleted documents will open up new blocks for possible future reuse. Since documents may keep internal references to different parts of the file, the in-place compact method will not always be able to recover lots of space.

If free space is a serious issue, and you have recently **deleted** a large number of documents or added more shards and **migrated data** away, the best approach is to trigger a *rolling initial sync* on every member of the shard one after another.

To check real storage space used for each member, loop through all databases, then run `db.stats()`, and add together the values of `storageSize` (which is the compressed data files without indexes) and `indexSize` (which is the total of all indexes from all collections on this database).

Key takeaways

From this chapter, the key concepts to remember are as follows:

- Sharding is a great way to expand write capacity in a deployment, but a good shard key is necessary to avoid excessive rebalancing through migration.

- Shard keys should include any unique constraint if that constraint must be maintained cluster-wide.

- Shard keys starting with incrementing values such as a date, timestamp, or `ObjectId` should be avoided since they lead to "hot shards" and rebalancing.

- Hashed shard keys can be good at distributing writes equally between shards, but make range queries inefficient.

- For import workloads (such as migrations from legacy databases), it can be more efficient to pre-split chunks and allow them to distribute evenly between shards before data loading.

- There are other tricks to predistribute chunks to avoid loading data into a "hot shard."

- Each database keeps its unsharded collections on a single shard, and it's possible to move these to another shard to fix shard imbalances.

- All operations to change shard configuration should be done via a `mongos`, with the balancer disabled and during scheduled maintenance windows to avoid unexpected application behavior.

CHAPTER 11

Extreme Sharding

This chapter goes even deeper into sharding specifics and introduces configurations that can increase write throughput when faced with hardware constraints. We also look at partitioning user data to adhere to data protection regulations, minimize costs, and optimize reads across shards.

Review

In most cases, a sharded cluster without zones or other size restrictions will automatically balance chunks of data by migrating them from a "heavy" shard with too many chunks to one with fewer chunks.

More shards

If you start hitting performance issues and have ruled out any application or schema design issues, a good option is to add more shards. This will offload data from the preexisting shards, lightening their workload and working set size in the memory cache.

A poor choice of shard key leading to hot shards (as described in Chapter 10) will not scale regardless of how many shards are added. Adding migration workload to a system already in distress will also make short-term performance worse.

If adding new hosts and shards is not an option, or if the current shards are not automatically balancing, then there can be certain manual adjustments made to force a more balanced workload.

Advanced chunk splitting

MongoDB will automatically trigger a split of large chunks during an insert into that chunk range or before migrating that chunk. We can force splits if we want to make certain chunks artificially smaller. Reasons for doing this might be that we are about to

© Nicholas Cottrell 2020
N. Cottrell, *MongoDB Topology Design*, https://doi.org/10.1007/978-1-4842-5817-0_11

import lots of data into that range and want to ensure that the inserts will be distributed more equally across all shards.

Once the split is done (either automatically or manually), the balancer may migrate that chunk to another shard. Remember that we can use `sh.status(true)` to see exactly where all chunks are currently stored.

There are two ways to manually split up a chunk:

- `sh.splitFind()` finds a chunk and splits it into two roughly equal chunks.

- `sh.splitAt()` finds a chunk with a given value and splits *exactly* at this point.

Let's make this clear with two examples. In Figure 11-1, we split a chunk with `sh.splitFind("myDb.customers", {custId: 9000})`. This first finds the chunk containing a document with customer ID of 9000 and then splits that chunks into two equal parts.

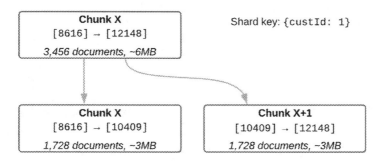

Figure 11-1. `splitFind` *splits into two roughly equals chunks*

In Figure 11-2, with `sh.splitAt("myDb.customers", {custId: 9000})`, that same chunk is split up at that exact value, giving us two chunks of very different sizes (600KB vs. 5MB). This might be appropriate if we're about to import some data into that point or need to control the shard of some special customers in that range.

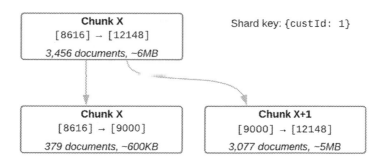

Figure 11-2. `splitAt` *splits exactly at the specified shard key value*

In terms of **performance**, `splitAt` is lighter weight and should be used in scripts when pre-splitting in preparation for data loading. `splitFind` tries to calculate the median point of values in the chunk to create equal size chunks. The fetching of documents and calculation requires both I/O and CPU.

Shard key scenarios

When choosing a shard key, there may be competing goals but not all of which can be satisfied in all cases. For example, we may want to optimize by reducing the *average load* of read queries, or we might want to reduce the *latency* of writes by using geolocated shards, or make *writes* of bulk data as fast as possible to complete by distributing writes most equally.

We'll examine each of these cases and review the best shard key and topology combinations.

Read performance

The absolute best way to ensure fast read responses in a sharded cluster is to only hit one shard. This means no waiting for the slowest shard, since there is no need to collate and sort the responses. But, how do we ensure we hit a single shard 99% of the time?

Let's imagine we have a database of all professional tennis players past and present. Table 11-1 shows what some typical documents in that database might look like.

Table 11-1. *Two sample documents from a large collection*

`{ _id: 123,`	`{ _id: 124,`
`  userName: "petesampras",`	`  userName: "bjornborg",`
`  country: "US",`	`  country: "SE",`
`  titles: 64,  .... }`	`  titles: 63,  .... }`

Based on the example documents, we could consider a number of shard keys such as

1. { userName: 1 }

2. { _id: "hashed" }

3. { country: 1, userName: 1 }

We wouldn't consider a simple { country: 1 } key since sharding on that basis could lead to jumbo chunks. That's because we could at most have about 195 chunks, one for each country.

We will need to perform many queries and aggregations on different combinations of fields, but it has been decided that the most important query to optimize is to sum the career titles of all players for a particular country. This query would look like the following:

```
db.players.aggregate([
  { $match: { country: "SE" } },
  { $group: {
    _id: "$country",
    count: { $sum: "$titles" }
    }
  }
]);
```

Let's first consider using {userName :1} as the shard key shown in Figure 11-3. For our aggregate call, we filter only on the country field, but since it's not part of the shard key, the documents could exist on any shard. Therefore, the mongos must query every single shard and then finally sum the titles once the slowest shard has responded. Note that Shard B ends up having no matches at all, but it still must do some work to determine that negative result.

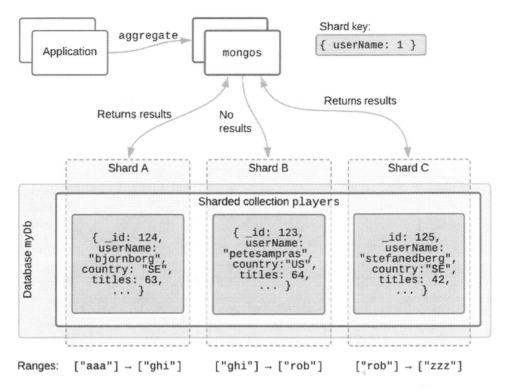

Figure 11-3. *Shard key forces all shards to be queried*

Sharding on {_id: "hashed"} would also hit every shard on any query not filtering on an exact equality match on the _id field. This makes it the worst choice when optimizing for read efficiency.

What if we sharded on {country:1, userName: 1} instead? In Figure 11-4, we see that because our shard key starts with country, we can narrow down to two shards that contain chunks with the country code of Sweden. In this case we need to wait for two shards to respond in order to make a final sum. Shard A can be ignored since there are no chunk ranges starting with the country code "SE" for Sweden.

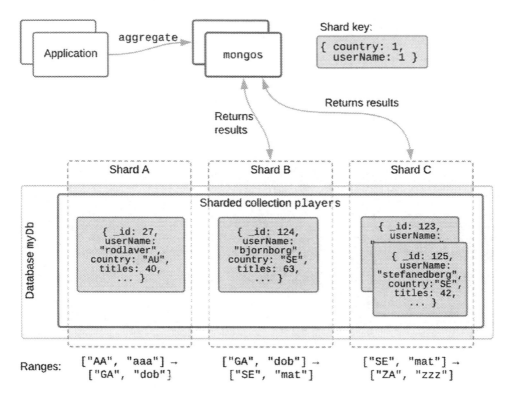

Figure 11-4. *Shard key is more targeted to the query*

Could we somehow ensure that only a single shard is targeted? Yes! We could use zone ranges and tags to achieve this. We could allocate one shard for European players ("EUR"), one for players from the Americas ("AMER"), and another for the rest of the world ("ROW").

We would have to define a key range for each and every country, for example:

```
sh.updateZoneKeyRange("myDb.players",
    { country: "SE", userName: MinKey },
    { country: "SE", userName: MaxKey }, "EUR")
```

and associate European players with Shard A:

```
sh.addShardToZone("shardA", "EUR")
```

While this is probably overkill for a relatively small database, the same technique could save valuable milliseconds on every query in a multi-terabyte sharded cluster.

Write performance

Let's imagine that we run a customer relationship management (CRM) solution for European paper sales company Wernham-Hogg. We are merging with US-based company Dunder Mifflin and need to import their entire customer data as efficiently as possible. In a sharded cluster, this can be achieved by distributing writes equally across our three shards.

Let's imagine the current European data is distributed approximately as shown in Figure 11-5 with the shard key {country:1, acct:1}. This is a simplified model and shows three sequential ranges, whereas in reality there will actually be many chunks inside each range.

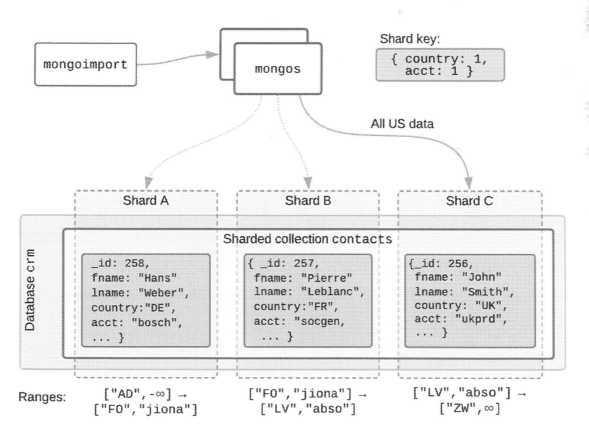

Figure 11-5. *A CRM with country-based sharding*

While this might not be the best shard key, it allows country-based analytics, eventual geo-sharding, and avoids jumbo chunks. Unfortunately, it also means that all the new data to import with {country: "US"} will all be sent to Shard C since it falls within the LV and ZW country code ranges.

Since Wernham-Hogg currently has almost no contacts in the CRM based on the United States, there will be just a single chunk containing those documents. If we were to import 100,000 contacts now, documents would be inserted into that one shard. As chunks grow they will be split into multiple smaller chunks. As more documents are inserted into those subchunks, they will be split over and over.

If the balancer is enabled, it will try migrating some chunks as that shard grows too large, but working in the background with low priority and with the pressure of the import, it will not have time to move many chunks, and the import will be effectively limited to a single shard.

The solution? We need to manually split these chunks in advance and distribute them evenly across the shards. If we already know roughly the distribution of account names from Dunder Mifflin's database, we could start with three big chunks and manually move those chunks so that each of the three shards has one chunk.

Then during import, the chunks will be automatically split. None of them will require migration since 1/3 of the data being imported will go to each shard.

We would like to distribute incoming data from the US contacts as shown in Table 11-2.

Table 11-2. *Our desired data distribution*

Values of account ID (lowercase)		Shard
Start	**End (inclusive)**	
a	m	A
l	q	B
r	z	C

To achieve the distribution in Table 11-1, we will use the sh.splitAt() function and ensure that we have three neat chunks starting with the letter "a" until "mzzzzzzz...", then another chunk starting from "l" until "qzzzzzzzz...", and a final chunk starting with "r", by declaring four boundaries as in Listing 11-1.

Listing 11-1. Creating four new chunks with an exact split point

```
sh.splitAt("crm.contacts", {country: "US", acct: "a"});
sh.splitAt("crm.contacts", {country: "US", acct: "l"});
sh.splitAt("crm.contacts", {country: "US", acct: "r"});
sh.splitAt("crm.contacts", {country: "US", acct: "zzzzzzzz"});
```

We then manually move these chunks with the sh.moveChunk() function by providing an example shard key value for a document which would exist inside these three chunks we just forced as shown in Listing 11-2.

Listing 11-2. Manually moving newly created chunks to other shards

```
sh.moveChunk("crm.contacts",
    {country: "US", acct: "abc"}, "shardA")
sh.moveChunk("crm.contacts",
    {country: "US", acct: "man"}, "shardB")
sh.moveChunk("crm.contacts",
    {country: "US", acct: "sta"}, "shardC")
```

We can confirm with sh.status() that the chunks have been migrated when the output looks like Listing 11-3.

Listing 11-3. Sharding status showing chunks on all three shards

```
databases:
  {  "_id" : "crm",  "primary" : "shardA",  "partitioned" : true,  ... } }
      crm.contacts
          shard key: { "country" : 1, "acct" : 1 }
          unique: true
          balancing: true
          chunks:
              shardA    2
              shardB    1
              shardC    2
                { "country" : { "$minKey" : 1 }, "acct" : { "$minKey" : 1 } } -->>
                { "country" : "US", "acct" : "a" } on : shardA Timestamp(2, 0)
```

```
{ "country" : "US", "acct" : "a" } -->> { "country" : "US",
"acct" : "l" } on : shardA Timestamp(3, 0)
{ "country" : "US", "acct" : "l" } -->> { "country" : "US",
"acct" : "r" } on : shardB Timestamp(4, 0)
{ "country" : "US", "acct" : "r" } -->> { "country" : "US",
"acct" : "zzzzzzzzzzz" } on : shardC Timestamp(4, 1)
{ "country" : "US", "acct" : "zzzzzzzzzzz" } -->> {
"country" : { "$maxKey" : 1 }, "acct" : { "$maxKey" : 1 } }
on : shardC Timestamp(1, 8)
```

We can now start our data loading, knowing that the write workload will be evenly distributed.

Multi-tenant architectures

MongoDB is a popular choice for building multi-tenant architectures and software-as-a-service (SaaS) applications. In some cases, the design chosen uses a *single database* with sharded collections to house all customers' data. This model typically uses a field in each document to identify the customer or project. Others chose to create a new *database per customer* and repeat the same collection names and indexes into each database.

Both approaches worked well with the original MMAP storage engine that simply mapped an in-memory data structure onto disk using native OS functionality. The number of files on disk scaled with the amount of data stored irrespective of the number of collections or indexes.

When the WiredTiger storage engine was introduced, the mapping of data files changed. Each collection was now stored in a single file on disk. Every index in each collection also was stored separately. Now multi-tenant architectures which were developed on the second model suddenly had many more separate files on disk.

File handles

Let's imagine a small multi-tenant cluster housing the databases for 24 tenants as well as a shared database for keeping system-wide metadata. We'll assume that each tenant database has 32 collections, and on average each collection has 3 indexes, making 96 indexes in each database. This gives 128 file handles required to load data from all these collections. If we are running this system against a replica set, during peak usage we could require up to 3200 file handles (24 databases × 128 file handles + the shared 128). Since each open file handle can take considerable memory resources, we start to hit a point where more memory is allocated to the OS for file descriptors than for keeping our MongoDB data in memory cache. You can imagine that a system that grows to thousands of tenants will suffer even more extremely from this effect.

In Figure 11-6, we see an example with the databases distributed over 6 shards instead. In this case, the nodes in each shard now only need up to 640 file handles open, compared to 3200.

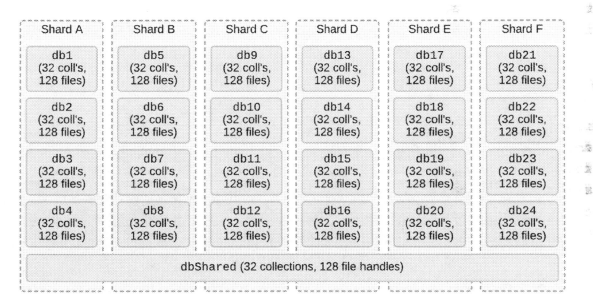

Figure 11-6. *Multi-tenant architecture with shards*

Virtual machines

With the availability of virtual machine technology, we would benefit from splitting up a single large host into multiple smaller virtual machines. We don't actually shard any collections, but ensure that the *primary shard* for each database is distributed evenly across the shards. As the number of tenants grows, we can add more shards to keep the total number of file handles to a reasonable maximum.

This added complexity for the cluster topology is not ideal, but it's often much easier to manage a large MongoDB cluster with the Enterprise automation tools than it is to completely reengineer a multi-tenant SaaS application.

Mixed architectures

With the increased popularity of cloud computing, even conservative enterprises with internal and legislated restrictions are moving operations to the cloud.

Often these cloud migrations are rolled out gradually from existing on-prem MongoDB nodes and applications. The first step is often moving arbiters to the cloud; then sometimes the cloud is used to provide a "third data center" when only two fully on-prem data centers are available.

Encryption

With the built-in support for encryption in transit and at rest and **field-level encryption,** even enterprises in the finance and healthcare sectors can be confident that data on the cloud is secure, even if they prefer to keep a majority of nodes on servers that they control directly.

Migrate services

The next phase is often moving out certain services to the cloud. For example, batch processing and analytics workloads may be kept on-prem, but customer-facing web or mobile services which need to be quickly scaled up and down several times a day due to usage patterns have a very strong cost-pressure to move to flexible cloud infrastructures.

Hidden costs

Moving applications to the cloud introduces a new cost source: **cloud bandwidth charges**. All of the major cloud providers charge for outgoing bytes from the cloud computing network. They usually also charge (but at a much lower rate) for data between availability zones. So even replica sets spread out over multiple availability zones in the same region will incur bandwidth charges for replication.

For enterprises, it's tempting to look for a way to reduce excessive bandwidth charges by reading from a node which is already co-located in the same zone. In theory this could mean only the replication bandwidth is required.

In Figure 11-7, we see a topology with primaries on-premise (since most of the write workload is still on-prem) but read replica members in the cloud. In certain cases, the cloud-based microservices could read from the cloud secondaries to avoid bandwidth charges, but will risk reading **stale data**.

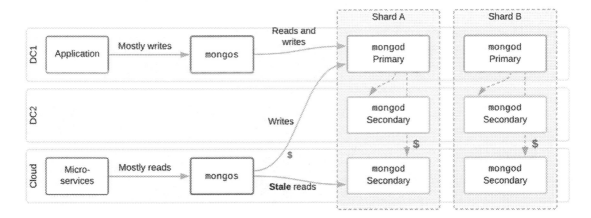

Figure 11-7. *Mixed deployment with primaries still on-prem*

Alternatively, as shown in Figure 11-8, the primaries could be located on the cloud. Now we may incur bandwidth charges for writes from the on-prem application. These writes will then need to be replicated back from the cloud to the other replica set members on-prem. *Replication chaining*, which is enabled by default, could be used to make the member in DC2 replicate from DC1.

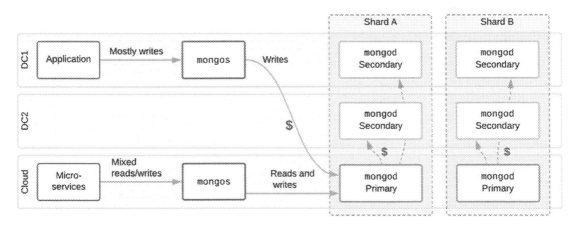

Figure 11-8. *Mixed deployment with primaries in the cloud*

Note   Network compression from applications to the mongos needs to be explicitly enabled by adding ?compressors=snappy to the Connection URI.

Policy restrictions

To complicate matters, there can still be certain cases where a selection of collections or entire databases from a sharded cluster cannot be stored on the cloud due to company policy or external regulations. In such situations, there are still some complex architectures that allow a cluster to have a significant number of cloud-based shards while keeping certain data always on-prem.

In Figure 11-9 we can see a sharded cluster with a confidential database whose content must be stored only in our own data centers. As long as all `confidential` collections are unsharded, they will remain on the primary Shard 3. If all replica set members for Shard 3 are in our data center, `confidential` data will never be stored in the cloud.

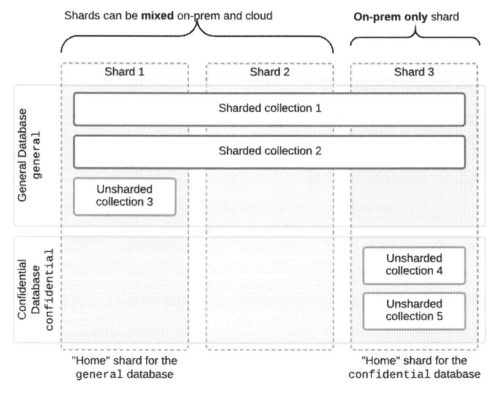

Figure 11-9. *A single cluster but with confidential data on-prem*

Replica set members for Shards 1 and 2 can be a mix of on-prem and cloud hosts like in Figures 11-7 and 11-8.

Scaling back a sharded cluster

In certain situations, you may have initially created a multi-shard cluster to prepare for the short-term growth of an application prior to big launch. But sometimes the data doesn't grow as fast as expected and some of that hardware can be better served in a different cluster or project.

Removing shards and freeing up hosts is reasonably straightforward. There are three major steps:

1. Relocate any data on that shard (specifically databases "homed" on that shard).

2. Remove any shard-level configuration referencing those shard nodes.

3. Shut down the nodes.

Relocating data

Let's imagine a simple example of a three-shard cluster with two databases, each with one sharded and one unsharded collection as shown in Figure 11-10. The database db2 is homed on Shard C, the shard we are about to remove.

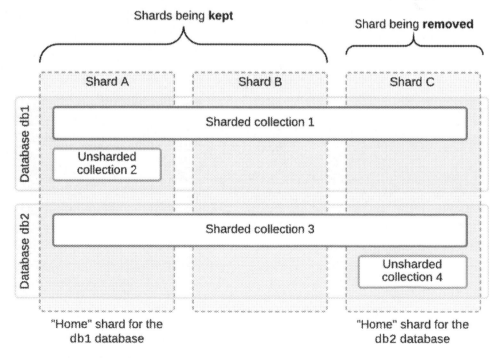

Figure 11-10. *A shard with homed databases pending draining*

Before Shard C can be *drained* of sharded collection data, we first need to choose a new location as the primary shard of db2. In this case, we should use Shard B to store the unsharded collections since Shard A is already home to db1 and this will help keep the shards balanced.

Maintenance window

Before starting any changes, we need to make sure that there are **no migrations active** and that there are **no read or write operations running** against the unsharded collections from db2. For safety, it is recommended to use a planned maintenance window and completely take down any applications using this database.

Move primary

Now we need to issue the following command via a mongos:

```
db.adminCommand( { movePrimary : "db2", to : "shardB" } )
```

This could take a considerable amount of time as the data needs to be transferred and then all the indexes on those unsharded collections are rebuilt on all members in the Shard B replica set.

Restart all components

Due to a known issue with the caching of metadata (up to an including at least version 4.2), it is now extremely important to

1. Restart all mongos instances and all mongod shard members (including the secondary members)

2. Connect to *all* mongos instances and *all* mongod shard members (including the secondary members) and run

   ```
   db.adminCommand({ flushRouterConfig: "db2" } )
   ```

Tip   Check https://jira.mongodb.org/browse/SERVER-17397 for the current best practices for your version of MongoDB.

Resume applications

Only once the router configuration has been flushed on all shard components, it is safe to relaunch any applications using this database.

Remove shard

Now that Shard C is no longer the primary shard for any databases, we can begin the removal process.

Drain shard

At this point, the unsharded collections have been moved, but there will still be portions of all sharded collections stored on Shard C. We will now move off all chunks of data from any database on Shard C, by connecting to a mongos and issuing the command:

```
db.adminCommand( { removeShard: "shardC" } )
```

You can run this command multiple times to check the status of the migration until it reports no chunks remaining on the shard. Now the collections will be located as per Figure 11-11.

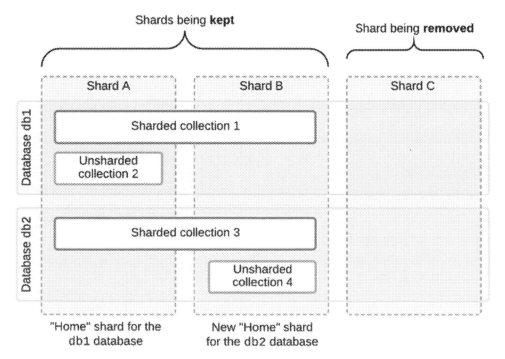

Figure 11-11. *A shard ready to be removed from the cluster*

Shut down shard

The replica set once comprising Shard C will still be operational but empty of any data, and no longer connected to the rest of the cluster's members. These isolated nodes can now be stopped and the hosts reused for other purposes.

Extremely large clusters

When clusters get very large with many chunk definitions and complex zoning rules, the size of the data on the config server replica set will naturally grow larger.

Each mongos keeps a cache of metadata about chunk locations and mapping to shards so that they can efficiently route queries to individual shards whenever possible. The memory requirements for this data will also grow for very large clusters, so mongos hosts may need to be upsized.

Config servers

It's also important to monitor both the disk space and performance of config servers particularly during the balancing window or intense data loading to ensure that they can cope with the workload.

For large clusters, it's better to run a five-member replica set for the config servers to help distribute read load from the mongoses and provide additional resiliency. You will also need to scale the CPU cores and memory of the config servers as the cluster grows, although generally only 2–4 cores would be required.

Key takeaways

From this chapter, the key concepts to remember are as follows:

- Shard keys can be chosen to optimize read performance for certain queries by avoiding "scatter-gather" queries which involve all shards.

- Splitting and migration of data during heavy data import is relatively slow and may mean all data hits a hot shard, greatly reducing performance and increasing total import time.

- Chunk ranges can be manually defined and distributed across chunks in order to optimize bulk loading of new data with known distribution of values.

- Chunks can be manually moved outside of the normal balancer window with a special admin command called `moveChunk`.

- Unsharded collections can be relocated to another shard by using the `movePrimary` command on their database.

- Draining an unneeded shard containing data can be initiated with the `removeShard` command.

- The cost of bandwidth between data centers and cloud providers differs greatly and can have a large effect on the total cost of running distributed clusters.

- Network communication between the application and `mongod`/`mongos` needs to be explicitly enabled in the connection URI.

- Databases can be homed on specific shards so that the physical location of unsharded collections can be controlled for regulatory or cost reasons.

Index

A

Access control, 191, 192

Access, restrict, 55, 56, 61

Arbiters, 31, 32

Atomicity, 7, 8

Auditing, 75, 86, 97

    logs, 67, 68

Authentication

    Active Directory, 176

    external, 62, 63, 176–178

    Kerberos, 61–63, 73

    keyfile, 59–61

    LDAP, 62, 63, 176, 177

    password, 59, 60

    SCRAM, 61, 63

    x509 certificate, 61

Authorization roles, 62

Automatic failure, 196

Automation tools, 153, 165, 249

Availability zone (AZ), 127, 183

B

Backups, 88, 89, 152

    encrypted, 66

    restoring from, 109

Balancer, 20, 21, 139, 140

Balancing, 231–235

Bandwidth, 126

    charges, 183, 185, 186

Binary JSON (BSON), 4

Bulk loading, 229, 230

C

Cardinality, 225

Certification, 73

Checkpoint, 10

Chunk

    distribution, 125, 136–143

    jumbo, 224, 225, 242, 246

    max size, 236

    migration, 125, 246

    range, 38, 239–241, 243, 245

    splitting, 125, 239–241

Cloud Manager, 152, 153

Cluster topology, 249

Collection

    capped, 14

    sharded, 248, 254, 255

    unsharded, 252–255

Compliance, 75–77, 82, 85, 89, 92, 93, 191

Compression, 185, 210

Concurrency, 4

Config server, 127, 139, 141, 256

Connection, 101, 102, 104, 115, 118–121

    management, 176, 177, 194

    pooling, 177

    timeout, 180–182

    URI, 40, 102

Consistency, 8, 175

© Nicholas Cottrell 2020
N. Cottrell, *MongoDB Topology Design*, https://doi.org/10.1007/978-1-4842-5817-0

Printed in the United States
By Bookmasters